Foundations of Canadian College English

Foundations of Canadian College English

Nadine Edwards

Bruce Evoy

Lawrence Hopperton

Teresa Reimann

Seneca College

Nelson Canada

I(T)P An International Thomson Publishing Company

Toronto • Albany • Bonn • Boston • Cincinnati • Detroit • London • Madrid • Melbourne
Mexico City • New York • Pacific Grove • Paris • San Francisco • Singapore • Tokyo • Washington

I(T)P™
International Thomson Publishing
The ITP logo is a trademark under licence

© Nelson Canada
A division of Thomson Canada Limited, 1996

Published in 1996 by
Nelson Canada
A division of Thomson Canada Limited
1120 Birchmount Road,
Scarborough, Ontario M1K 5G4

Canadian Cataloguing in Publication Data

Main entry under title:

Foundations of Canadian college English

ISBN 0-17-605551-7

1. English language – Grammar.   I. Edwards, Nadine.

PEII12.F68   1996   428.5   C95-933147-6

Publisher and Team Leader	Michael Young
Acquisitions Editor	Andrew Livingston
Production Editor	Tracy Bordian
Project Coordinator	Joanne Scattolon
Production Coordinator	Brad Horning
Administrative Coordinator	Evan Turner
Art Director	Liz Harasymczuk
Cover Design	Julie Greener
Composition	VISU*TronX*
Input Analyst	June Reynolds

Printed and bound in Canada

1 2 3 4 (WC) 98 97 96 95

CONTENTS

Module 10 — Punctuation and Capitalization   177

Module 11 — Paragraphs   199

ACKNOWLEDGMENTS

This text is the combined efforts of a dedicated and talented group of educators. I would like to take this opportunity to thank them for their enthusiastic contributions as developers, reviewers, and testers of the manuscript. Thanks must go to the following reviewers: Nathan Greenfield (Algonquin College), Joseph Kertes (Humber College), Pat Rogin (Durham College), Brian Thwaits (Mohawk College), and V. Lynn Whelan (Georgian College). In addition, I would like to thank Anna Czajkowski, Cecile Goodman, Gail Henderson, Sharon Lahaye, Earl Molyneaux, and Pearl Owens. Without their efforts and cooperation, nothing could have been accomplished.

I would like to thank the students of English Upgrading in 1994 and 1995 who tested the manuscript in regular classroom, individualized learning, and distance delivery modes, and commented upon its strengths and weaknesses.

Lastly, I would like to thank the administrative team of the Faculty of Continuing Education, specifically Richard Grannan, Cindy Hazell, Anthony Tanner, David McHardy, and Al Woodward, who believed in this project, fought for it, and secured the funding necessary for its development.

Truly this has been a team effort, and every member of the team deserves far more praise than I can give in this limited space. It has been a privilege to work with this team on this project and coordinate the English subjects in the Faculty of Continuing Education of Seneca College. I am constantly impressed with the dedication and the abilities of our faculty.

Larry Hopperton, Coordinator
Faculty of Continuing Education
Seneca College of Applied Arts and Technology

INTRODUCTION

This textbook will introduce you to the principles of written English. Writing demands clarity, conciseness, and precision. The source of these is a solid command of the rules of English grammar. Think about grammar as the building blocks for effective written communication.

In constructing a brick wall, every brick must be put into its right place. Each brick must be solid and perfectly cemented or the wall will fall. Correct grammatical structures are the bricks of communication. Your own critical and analytical thinking is the mortar that will hold your wall together. As the wall is being built, layer upon layer of bricks are added until the structure has been completed.

As teachers, we often hear students say, "But you know what I mean." Our answer is consistent: "I know what you have written, but I cannot guess at your meaning. You must be explicit and clear because I may guess wrongly." Mastering the tools of language covered in this text will help you achieve clarity in your writing.

In 1992, the Conference Board of Canada, a consulting group made up of some of the largest employers in this country, issued a report called *Employability Skills Profile* in which it discussed the requirements of the work force of the future. While the document does discuss personal management and teamwork skills, it states that the most critical skill required of the Canadian work force is communication abilities. These skills are specified as follows:

- the ability to listen, learn, and to understand;
- the ability to read, comprehend, and use written materials; and
- the ability to write effectively in the language of business.

Mastering the building blocks of written English will help you with each of these skills. A sound understanding of language will help you read and learn by focusing your attention on the most important aspects of your texts and your classroom lessons. It will also help you to achieve clarity in your writing so that you can explain yourself clearly and confidently to both instructors and business contacts. This, in turn, should lead to success in your studies and your career. According to the industries for which you will be working, your ability to succeed in your chosen profession is directly related to your ability to communicate.

USING THIS TEXTBOOK

Education is more than a process of dispensing information to students who try to memorize the right answer. Education is about learning to think within a universe of discourse. Our universe, within this textbook, is written English.

You will find that there is more involved in education than simply finding the "right" answer. As you work with this book, you will be continually asked to explain your answers. Since education is about thinking, we want to know *why* you think an answer is correct. This will let your teachers help you to understand this universe of discourse. This is the overall goal not only of this subject, but also of education as a whole.

This text is made up of a series of self-contained modules. You will notice that every module begins with a *Learning Outcome* statement, which specifies how you will demonstrate your mastery of the module lessons. We have included many exercises, and answers to the odd-numbered exercises at the back of the module. Work through all of these. If your answers do not coincide with those at the back, ask your instructor to explain the errors.

There are some basic tools that every person should have. These are a good dictionary and a handbook of grammar and usage. Both of these are available in most bookstores. Buy them, and keep them handy at all times.

Always remember that although your education is your right, rights also imply responsibilities. Nobody is responsible for your education except you; nobody can learn for you. If you have questions, ask for answers. If you get an exercise wrong, ask your instructor to explain things until they are clear to you. It is not up to you to keep your teacher happy; rather, it is up to your teacher to help you to learn. You are the most important person in this process. Your teachers will work for you if you tell them what you need. They will do everything they can to help you succeed, but, ultimately, your education is up to you.

Use a pencil as you work through this book. Writing in pencil allows you to draft your responses to questions, and to change those answers that are incorrect.

SENTENCES: A FIRST LESSON

From the first module, you will be asked to write a sentence to explain your answer. While the details of sentences will be discussed in Module 9, all you need to know right now, in order to get started, is that a sentence is made up of two things:

- a *subject* (the person, place, thing, or idea that does something)
- a *predicate* or *verb* (the action that is taking place)

Consider the following examples:

1. I think the answer is 7.
   I is the person doing the thinking, and the action that *I* is doing is thinking.

2. Nguyen is from Korea.
   Nguyen is the person in this sentence about whom a statement is being made. *Is from Korea* is a statement.

3. Ranbir works in the payroll office.
   Ranbir is the person doing the action. The action being done is *working*.

4. Sometimes, I have trouble understanding the rules of grammar.
   I is the person doing the action. *Have* expresses the action of *I*.

Full sentences are really quite easy to write. Every time you write one, ask yourself the following questions:

- Who or what is the person, place, thing, or idea that is doing something?
- What is it doing?

How do you know that your sentences make sense? Try the ear test. Say your sentence out loud to someone. Does it *sound* right to you? Does it *make sense* to them? If it sounds right, then the chances are high that it *is* right. If it sounds a little strange, back up a step and ask yourself about the subject and the predicate. Are these clear?

Your instructor will want you to give your answers in complete sentences. Module 9 will discuss sentences at length, but this is enough of a starting point for you.

We hope that you enjoy this subject and that you master its lessons. If you have any problems, make sure that your instructor explains things to your satisfaction.

COMMON ERROR INDEX

Below is a list of some of the most common errors made in grammar. The modules and sections in which the errors are located are listed below.

In addition to this general, common error index, you should remember that every person makes their own common errors. As you work through this text, you should build your Personal Common Error Index. This will help you to become aware of your own difficulties and how to correct them.

PERSONAL COMMON ERROR INDEX

Module	**Type**	**Page**

ENGLISH PLACEMENT TEST

INTRODUCTION

Before you begin to work through this textbook, take this diagnostic test. Each of the main elements or "building blocks" of English grammar is addressed in a separate module. This test will identify the modules on which you need to concentrate.

Work through the test and try to complete as much of it as you can. Do not worry about the modules that you do not understand. Remember, this is not a pass/fail situation; the purpose of this test is to establish your present level of knowledge so that you can use this textbook to focus on *your* areas of weakness.

Your instructor will mark this test and discuss the results with you. If you have made two or more errors in a module section, you should try the pre-test that your instructor will provide. This test will indicate the areas within the module on which you need to focus in order to meet the Learning Outcome of that module.

Well, let's get started!

MODULE 1

1.1   In each blank write the plural form for each of the following nouns:

1. knife _____

2. inventory _____

3. goose _____

4. mouse _____

5. father-in-law _____

6. sheep _____

7. scissors _____

8. attorney-at-law _____

MODULE 2

2.1   Underline the correct pronoun from the pair in the brackets.

1. (It's, Its) a great city for food.

2. I shall give the letter to (whoever, whomever) claims it.

3, (Who, Whom) did you tell about this fine restaurant?

4. Tim, Shu-Fen, and (her, she) bought coffee and muffins.

5. (Her, She) and Mary take the bus to school every day.

6. The cat stepped on (it's, its) tail.

MODULE 3

3.1   The verbs in the following sentences are incorrectly used. Rewrite the sentences, replacing the incorrect verb with the correct form.

1. Have you took notes of what she told you?

_____

2. He do not need to go.

_____

3. On my desk is four letters that must be mailed today.

_____

4. The success of direct mail campaigns seems certain.

_____

5. There is too many mistakes in this letter.

_____

6. Neither the book nor the play are interesting.

_____

7. The club has chose Miss Lam as chairperson.

_____

8. One of my favourite programs were cancelled.

_____

MODULE 4

4.1   Some of these sentences contain adjective or adverb errors. Rewrite the sentences and make corrections where necessary.

1. Conrad Black is one of the most richest men in Canada.

_____

2. Which of the twins has the best personality?

_____

3. Smoking is the lesser of the two evils.

_____

4. He sat quiet through the ceremony.

_____

5. The company picnic was a real big success.

_____

4.2   Identify the adjectives in the following sentences:

1. That large crowd of excited people is waiting patiently.

_____

2. The group has been waiting in line for an hour.

_____

3. They will feel happy when they have bought their tickets to the music concert.

_____

4.3   Identify the adverbs in the following sentence.

1. Yesterday, at the outdoor concert, the band played very well.

_____

MODULE 5

5.1   Write a series of sentences using the verb _play_ as a present participle, a past participle, a present perfect participle, and a gerund.

Present participle:

_____

Past participle:

_____

Present perfect participle:

_____

Gerund:

_____

MODULE 6

6.1   In the following sentences underline the conjunctions once and the prepositions twice:

1. Cats and dogs are common pets.

2. Would you like peas or corn with your dinner?

3. We will not travel outside the country because of the exchange rate on the dollar.

4. She is not only an interesting person but also a good friend.

MODULE 7

7.1   In the following sentences use square brackets to show any adjective phrases and use curved brackets to show any adverb phrases. Draw arrows to show the part of speech that each phrase modifies:

1. Police in squad cars cruised along the highway.

2. In hot weather fish remain in the deep water.

3. Crowds of people rush to the beach on the weekends.

4. Swarms of insects buzzed around the light.

5. With a sly smile he winked at his partner.

7.2 In the following sentences underline any prepositional phrases.

1. They looked toward us.

2. The kitten was hiding under a basket in the grass.

3. I was kept in suspense throughout the entire story.

4. The trees growing by the river are willows.

5. Are you looking for me?

MODULE 8

8.1 Underline the main clause once and the subordinate clause twice in the following sentences.

1. Since her father worked there, she knew the school.

2. Never eat fruit that is not washed first.

3. I will not go unless you go with me.

4. She stayed in the game because she was needed.

5. After the game was over, we went out for pizza.

MODULE 9

9.1 Indicate whether the following sentences are complete or incomplete by writing *C* beside the complete sentences and *INC* beside the incomplete sentences. Write a sentence in which you explain each of your answers.

1. Most companies give us prompt and efficient service.

_____

2. As soon as you have completed the exercises assigned by the instructor.

_____

3. To insert the paper properly in the printer.

_____

4. The final show rates as the outstanding event of the year.

_____

5. Who is an administrative assistant, earned her diploma at Seneca College.

_____

9.2 In each sentence, underline the complete subject once, and the complete predicate twice.

1. The long winter days passed slowly.

2. Betty visited the CBC television studio.

3. The plane left two hours late.

4. Did you go?

5. A group of school children went to the zoo.

MODULE 10

10.1 Rewrite the following sentences, correcting the capitalization and punctuation errors.

1. who was elvis presley

_____

2. if the buses go on strike I shall not be able to get to work.

_____

3. when he went to toronto mr leung visited the skyDome maple leaf gardens casa loma and the CNE

_____

4. mr brown our english teacher is retiring

_____

5. his play opened on april 23 1991 and closed on may 26 1991

_____

6. tie your shoelaces

_____

7. on her business trip kim stopped at montreal quebec toronto ontario regina saskatchewan and vancouver british columbia

_____

8. we have some difficulties with english grammar therefore we are taking this subject

_____

MODULE 11

Write a paragraph (approximately 200 words) about one event that has had a significant influence on your life.

_____

_____

_____

_____

MODULE 1

NOUNS

Learning Outcome Statement

By successfully completing a series of module exercises, you will be able to identify nouns and their uses and to write sentences using nouns correctly.

NOUNS

1.1 WHAT IS A NOUN?

A **noun** is simply the name of a person, place, or thing. These are called **concrete nouns**. Nouns are also the names of ideas or qualities. These are called **abstract nouns**.

Person:	Mary	Hassan	girl	boy
Place:	Halifax	classroom	school	beach
Thing:	book	computer	car	table
Idea:	freedom	liberation	thought	justice
	love	happiness	anger	courage

Let us look at the wide range of nouns used in the following sentences:

1. *Mr. Armstrong*, the *architect* of that *house*, used great *imagination* in the *construction* of an *arch* in the *garden*.

2. A *drive* to the *country* in a *jeep* gives *Jelissa* a magnificent *sense* of *freedom*.

The nouns are indicated with *italic text*. What type of noun is each italicized word?

EXERCISE 1.1

Underline the nouns in the following sentences.

1. Alison will send two copies of the report to the supervisor.

2. The papers are lying on the desk.

3. The boys rode their bicycles to school.

4. Scientists found a skull buried in the sand.

5. The baker made five dozen cookies for the party.

1.2 KINDS OF NOUNS

Nouns are classified in several ways: common nouns (which include concrete and abstract nouns), proper nouns, and collective nouns.

Common nouns name persons, places, or things in general terms. Common nouns do not begin with capital letters.

The *parents* watched a *movie* in the *classroom*.

Parents, *movie*, and *classroom* are general terms not naming anyone or anything in particular. These are considered to be common nouns.

Common nouns are either concrete or abstract. **Concrete nouns** name things you can see, hear, smell, touch, or taste, such as a tree, the sunrise, or the wind. **Abstract nouns** refer to ideas or qualities that cannot be seen, heard, touched, smelled, or tasted, such as happiness, love, and strength.

Proper nouns are names of people, places, or things and begin with capital letters.

Kevin Tran attended *Capilano College*.

Kevin Tran, the name of a specific person, is a proper noun. *Capilano College,* the name of a particular place, is also a proper noun.

Collective nouns are names of groups of persons or objects, for example:

committee	majority	team
audience	company	flock

Collective nouns may take either the singular (meaning one only) or plural (meaning more than one), depending on their use in a sentence. If a collective noun refers to the group acting as a whole or a unit, the noun takes a singular verb. Verbs will be discussed in Module 3.

The *staff meets* every morning for coffee.

staff—collective noun
meets—singular verb

If a collective noun refers to a group in which the members act individually, the noun takes a plural verb.

The *group have given* their consent for an outside picnic.

group—collective noun
have given—plural verb

Parts of numbers or sums of money are also collective nouns, for example, *$100*, *three-fifths*, *one-third*.

One-third of the class went for lunch.

one-third (part of a number)—collective noun
class (name of a group of people)—collective noun

My money is on the table.

money—collective noun

FREQUENTLY USED COLLECTIVE NOUNS

These nouns refer to collections of individuals:

army	company	herd	panel
assembly	congregation	jury	police
audience	crew	majority	public
band	crowd	mass	school
cast	faculty	mob	staff
choir	family	nation	swarm
class	flock	navy	team
club	gang	number	
committee	group	orchestra	

EXERCISE 1.2.1

Underline all the nouns in the following sentences and state the kinds of each. In the case of a common noun, state if it is concrete or abstract.

1. Your daughter says she wants to be a doctor. _____

2. All prejudices are harmful. _____

3. Trout is my favourite main course. _____

4. Which movie do you prefer, *The Firm* or *The Bodyguard*? _____

5. Honesty is the best policy. _____

EXERCISE 1.2.2

Write sentences using all the kinds of nouns.

1. Common (abstract): _____

2. Proper: _____

3. Common (concrete): _____

4. Collective: _____

1.3 USES OF NOUNS IN SENTENCES (RELATION)

Nouns are found in various positions in a sentence. They may be subjects or objects of verbs, objects of prepositions, or complements.

> *NOTE:* A sentence is a group of words that must contain both a subject and a verb.

NOUNS AS SUBJECTS

Every sentence is organized around a subject. To find the subject of any sentence, ask yourself this question: *Whom or what is the sentence about?* When you have answered this question, you have found the subject of the sentence.

Carla works.	Whom or what is the sentence about? This sentence is about Carla; therefore, *Carla* is the subject.
Justice prevailed.	Whom or what is this sentence about? This sentence is about justice; therefore, the subject is *justice*.

NOUNS AS OBJECTS

In the previous sentences, a verb, the word that states the action, was enough to complete a statement about the subject. Many actions cannot complete a sentence by themselves and require objects to receive the action they express.

Noun objects of verbs are of two kinds: direct and indirect.

1. Direct Object (of a verb)

How do you find a direct object? Ask the verb the questions "Whom?" or "What?" The noun answer will be the direct object.

■ **Examples:**

> I visited my sister yesterday.

In this sentence the verb is *visited*. The question to ask the verb is "visited whom?" The answer is *my sister*. *Sister* is therefore the direct object of the verb *visited*.

> I watched the show with great pleasure.

In this sentence the verb is *watched*. The question to ask the verb is, "watched what?" The answer is *the show*. *Show* is therefore the direct object of the verb *watched*.

2. Indirect Object (of a verb)

To find the indirect object of the verb, ask the verb the question "to whom?" The noun answer will be the indirect object of the verb.

■ **Examples:**

> I gave my mother flowers on her birthday.

"To whom" did you give the flowers? You gave your *mother* the flowers; therefore, *mother* is the indirect object of the verb.

> He brought the teacher an apple.

"To whom" did he bring the apple? He brought the *teacher* an apple; therefore, *teacher* is the indirect object of the verb.

NOUNS AS OBJECTS OF PREPOSITIONS

When a noun follows a preposition, that noun is the object of the preposition. A preposition is a word that starts a phrase. (Prepositions will be discussed in Module 6; phrases in Module 7.) You will find objects of the preposition by asking the preposition "whom?" or "what?" The noun that answers this question will be the object of the preposition.

> He is a relative of the *manager*.

Using the preposition *of*, ask the question "of whom?" The answer is *manager*. Hence, *manager* is the object of the preposition *of*.

> Park the car in the *driveway*.

Using the preposition *in*, ask the question "in what?" The answer is *driveway*. Thus, *driveway* is the object of the preposition *in*.

NOUNS AS COMPLEMENTS

Some verbs (*to be*, *become*, *seem*, *appear*, and *feel*) express a state of being instead of action. Such verbs take a noun as a subject **complement**, rather than an object, to complete their meaning.

■ **Examples:**

Mary is a *teacher*.

John became a *minister*.

That boy is a *leader*.

> *NOTE:* The complement refers directly to the subject. *Teacher* complements *Mary* because *Mary* and *teacher* are the same person. In fact, *teacher* is linked to the subject by the linking verb *is*. Also note that the complement and the subject are the same person or thing, simply expressed by different nouns.

EXERCISE 1.3.1

a) Circle all nouns in the following sentences.
b) State how each is being used: as subject, object of the verb, object of the preposition, or complement.

1. Antonio went into the store where he bought a doll for his little daughter.

2. During the night there was a heavy rainfall.

3. Helen is the leader of the group.

4. When are the Rolling Stones coming to town?

5. Can you get tickets to the concert?

EXERCISE 1.3.2

Rewrite the following sentences, underlining all the direct objects once, and all indirect objects twice.

1. Jose bought his daughter a doll.

2. The teacher taught his students fractions.

3. Sheila showed her aunt a homemade videotape.

4. Did your boyfriend give his brother a gift for Hanukkah?

5. What present did you buy your mother for Easter?

1.4 THE NUMBER OF NOUNS

A noun may be singular or plural. A noun that refers to one person, place, or thing is singular in number. A noun that refers to more than one person, place, or thing is plural in number.

Some general rules for the endings of plural nouns follow.

PLURALS FORMED BY ADDING *S*

The plurals of most nouns are formed by adding *s* to the singular form:

boy	boys	desk	desks
manager	managers	bank	banks
idea	ideas	German	Germans

Nouns ending in *o* or *y* preceded by a vowel also form plurals by adding *s*:

radio	radios	studio	studios
valley	valleys	day	days

A few nouns ending in *o* preceded by a consonant form their plurals by adding *s*. And *all* musical terms ending in *o*, regardless of the letter preceding the *o*, merely add *s* to form the plural:

auto	autos	piano	pianos

Some nouns ending in *f*, *fe*, or *ff* form their plurals by simply adding *s*.

proof	proofs	chief	chiefs
safe	safes	cliff	cliffs
belief	beliefs	briefs	briefs

NOTE: Many of the above nouns simply have to be memorized. If in doubt, consult your dictionary.

PLURALS FORMED BY ADDING *ES*

Nouns ending in *s*, *ch*, *sh*, *x*, and *z* form the plural by adding *es*. The sound of the extra "e" is needed both for smoothness between the two "s" sounds and to distinguish the singular form from the plural form. This will usually give the word an extra syllable. An easy test for this spelling is for you to say the singular and plural forms of the word out loud. If there is an extra syllable in the plural form of the word, it probably ends with *es*.

business	businesses	bus	buses
church	churches	branch	branches

Nouns ending in *o* and preceded by a consonant most often form their plurals by adding *es*.

echo	echoes	cargo	cargoes
hero	heroes	potato	potatoes
tomato	tomatoes	motto	mottoes

PLURALS FORMED BY CHANGING *Y* TO *I*, OR *F* AND *FE* TO *V*, BEFORE ADDING *ES*

Some nouns ending in *y* preceded by a consonant form their plurals by changing *y* to *i* and adding *es*:

factory	factories
company	companies
quantity	quantities

Some nouns change the *f* or *fe* to *v* and add *es*:

wife	wives	knife	knives
loaf	loaves	shelf	shelves

Some nouns form their plurals by a *change in the spelling*:

man	men	tooth	teeth
goose	geese	mouse	mice

A few nouns use *n* or *en* to form their plural:

ox	oxen	child	children

With compound nouns the more important word is usually pluralized:

father-in-law	*fathers*-in-law
chief-of-staff	*chiefs*-of-staff
governor-general	*governors*-general

Some nouns are plural in form but singular in meaning, and therefore take singular verbs (see Module 3):

news, series, mumps, measles, civics, physics, mathematics, politics

Other nouns are always considered plural in form, and take plural verbs (see Module 3):

trousers, pants, scissors, shears, eye-glasses, headquarters, proceeds, riches, thanks

A few nouns are spelled the same way in both the singular and plural forms:

sheep, deer, moose, trout, salmon

Letters, figures, and words used as words form their plural by adding an apostrophe and *s* (*'s*).

p's, 9's, and's

Watch your p's and q's.

There are too many and's in your essay.

IRREGULAR PLURALS

Many English words are taken directly from other languages. Some of these borrowed words retain the plural form used in the original language.

For words ending in *us* change to *i*:

radius	radii
stimulus	stimuli
fungus	fungi

For words ending in *is* the plural form is *es*:

crisis	crises
parenthesis	parentheses
basis	bases
hypothesis	hypotheses

EXERCISE 1.4.1

Write the plural form of the following nouns in the space provided.

1. factory	_____	9. louse	_____
2. axis	_____	10. alley	_____
3. half	_____	11. boss	_____
4. foot	_____	12. tattoo	_____
5. lottery	_____	13. toothbrush	_____
6. piano	_____	14. tray	_____
7. sheep	_____	15. monkey	_____
8. ally	_____	16. p	_____

EXERCISE 1.4.2

Write the singular form of the following nouns in the space provided.

1. wolves	_____	9. stories	_____
2. ponies	_____	10. geese	_____
3. remedies	_____	11. allies	_____
4. chimneys	_____	12. children	_____
5. sons-in-law	_____	13. spoonfuls	_____
6. roofs	_____	14. leaves	_____
7. mice	_____	15. oases	_____
8. wrenches	_____	16. deer	_____

1.5   CASE OF NOUNS

Case is a term used to indicate the form or position of a noun or pronoun in a sentence. (Pronouns will be discussed in Module 2.) It shows the noun/pronoun's use or relationship to other words in that sentence. In English, there are three cases for nouns: subjective, possessive, and objective.

Subjects of sentences and complements following linking verbs are in the *subjective case*. These have already been discussed under the heading "Uses of Nouns in Sentences."

Nouns showing possession or ownership are in the *possessive case* (see below). Nouns used as direct objects, indirect objects, or objects of prepositions are in the *objective case*.

1.6   POSSESSIVES

Nouns become possessive when they show ownership or possession. To show ownership or possession, we can use such words as *belongs to*, *owned by*, or (most commonly) *of:*

> The car that *belongs to* Nguyen
>
> The car *owned by* Nguyen
>
> The car *of* Nguyen

To indicate a possessive form, add an apostrophe and *s* (*'s*) or an *apostrophe alone* ('):

> Mark's car   Charles' horse

Add *'s* to singular and plural nouns that do not end in *s:*

> singular: boy's dog   the horse's hoof
> plural: men's room   children's toys

Add only an apostrophe (') to plural and singular nouns that end in *s:*

> singular: Moses' laws   Mr. Jones' temper
> plural: the Joneses' house the ladies' coats

Add an apostrophe and *s* (*'s*) to the last word of compound nouns:

> singular: mother-in-law's   chief-of-staff's
> plural: mothers-in-law's   chiefs-of-staff's

Add an apostrophe and *s* (*'s*) to an organizational name at the end of the complete name, even if the final word is an abbreviation:

> IBM's computers   Esso Oil Company's refineries

Add an apostrophe and *s* (*'s*) only to the last name to indicate joint ownership:

> Kara and Fernando's cottage   The cottage jointly belongs to Kara and to Fernando. (one owner)

Add an apostrophe and *s* (*'s*) to each name to indicate individual ownership.

> John's and Thuy's boats   There are two boats: one belongs to John and the other belongs to Thuy. (two owners)

> *NOTE:* Never use an apostrophe when forming the plural of a noun. It is incorrect to write: "Jim has two son's."

EXERCISE 1.6.1

Write the singular possessive and plural possessive of each of the following expressions.

	Singular Possessive	**Plural Possessive**
1. the tail of the cat	_____	_____
2. the pen of the writer	_____	_____
3. the robes of the monarch	_____	_____
4. the fur of the lady	_____	_____
5. the toes of the child	_____	_____

EXERCISE 1.6.2

In each sentence, find the noun that requires an apostrophe ('). Rewrite all sentences, adding apostrophes where they are needed.

1. The soldiers uniforms were dirty.

_____

2. Running and swimming were my daughters favourite exercises.

_____

3. Ron and Hsiu food supply is running out. (joint ownership)

_____

4. The mens hockey sticks were broken.

_____

5. Kohai Yamanas three travel agents were busy.

_____

EXERCISE 1.6.3

In the following sentences, underline once all nouns in the subjective case. Underline twice all nouns in the possessive case. Circle all nouns in the objective case.

1. Excessive snow froze the ground.

2. Please pay for my sister's work.

3. They lent their fellow students some books.

4. My brother sold Len some tulips.

5. How many legs does a giraffe have?

EXERCISE 1.6.4

Give the case and relation of the underlined nouns in each of the following sentences.

1. <u>Miss Cheng</u> gave us a lot of <u>homework</u>.

_____

2. The <u>boys</u> liked the <u>captain</u> of their <u>team</u>.

_____

3. The <u>milkman</u> gave <u>Janet</u> five <u>dollars</u> in <u>loonies</u>.

_____

4. The <u>man</u> who used to live on the next <u>block</u> became a brilliant <u>lawyer</u>.

_____

5. The <u>cream</u> in <u>Bill's</u> <u>coffee</u> curdled.

_____

SOME SPECIAL POSSESSIVES

Nouns that designate time are frequently used in the possessive form:

a minute's notice   one year's vacation

two weeks' pay   three hours' work

A noun following a possessive form may not appear in the sentence but is understood:

I am going to the doctor's. (doctor's office)

Please pick up my suit at Eaton's. (Eaton's department store)

ANSWER KEY

EXERCISE 1.1

1. Alison, copies, reports, supervisor
3. boys, bicycles, school
5. baker, cookies, party

EXERCISE 1.2.1

1. *daughter*—common, concrete; *doctor*—common, concrete
3. *trout*—common, concrete; *course*—common, abstract
5. *honesty*—common, abstract; *policy*—common, abstract

EXERCISE 1.2.2

Sentences will vary.

EXERCISE 1.3.1

1. *Antonio*, subject; *store*, object of the preposition; *doll*, object of the verb; *daughter*, object of the preposition
3. *Helen*, subject; *leader*, complement; *group*, object of the preposition
5. *tickets*, object of the verb; *concert*, object of the preposition

EXERCISE 1.3.2

1. Jose bought his <u>daughter</u> a <u>doll</u>.
3. Sheila showed her <u>aunt</u> a homemade <u>videotape</u>.
5. What <u>present</u> did you buy your <u>mother</u> for Easter?

EXERCISE 1.4.1

1. factories	3. halves	5. lotteries	7. sheep
9. lice	11. bosses	13. toothbrushes	15. monkeys

EXERCISE 1.4.2

1. wolf	3. remedy	5. son-in-law	7. mouse
9. story	11. ally	13. spoonful	15. oasis

EXERCISE 1.6.1

1. cat's tail; cats' tails
3. monarch's robes; monarchs' robes
5. child's toes; children's toes

EXERCISE 1.6.2

1. The soldiers' uniforms were dirty.
3. Ron and Hsiu's food supply is running out.
5. Kohai Yamanas' three travel agencies are busy.

EXERCISE 1.6.3

1. Excessive <u>snow</u> froze the (ground.)
3. They lent their fellow students some (books.)
5. How many (legs) does a <u>giraffe</u> have?

EXERCISE 1.6.4

1. *Miss Cheng* subjective, subject of the verb *gave*
   homework, objective, object of the preposition *of*
3. *milkman*, subjective, subject of the verb *gave*
   Janet, objective, indirect object of the verb *gave*
   dollars, objective, direct object of the verb *gave*
   loonies, objective, object of the preposition *in*
5. *cream*, subjective, subject of the verb *curdled*
   Bill's, possessive
   coffee, objective, object of the preposition *in*

MODULE  2

PRONOUNS

Learning Outcome Statement

By successfully completing a series of module exercises, you will be able to identify and use pronouns correctly and to classify them with regard to kind, number, person, case, and relation.

PRONOUNS

2.1   WHAT IS A PRONOUN?

A **pronoun** is a word that takes the place of a noun; it replaces a word that names someone or something. By using pronouns, we can talk about someone or something without repeating the same noun over and over again.

■ **Examples:**

Mr. Buckley warned Sylvia and Marjorie not to touch *his* budgie because *it* might bite *them*.

Mrs. Afroze asked Tamara to stay after hockey practice so that *she* could work with *her* on *her* shots.

This is what would happen if the pronouns were not used:

Mr. Buckley warned Sylvia and Marjorie not to touch *Mr. Buckley's* budgie because *the budgie* might bite *Sylvia and Marjorie*.

Mrs. Afroze asked Tamara to stay after hockey practice so that Mrs. Jamieson could work with Tamara on Tamara's shots.

Sentences are much smoother and tighter in style when nouns are replaced with pronouns.

EXERCISE 2.1.1

Identify each pronoun in the following sentences and also the noun that each has replaced. State your answers in complete sentences as in the example below.

■ **Example:**

"Jeremy, would *you* please wash the dishes for *me*," said Emily.

The word *you* has replaced *Jeremy*, and the word *me* has replaced *Emily*.

1.   Janine twisted an ankle while she was figure skating.

2.   Henry and Marcus asked Mr. Cauley if he would help them.

3.   "Mrs. Kwak told us to wait until she came back," replied the girls.

4.   Samantha cannot ride the new bicycle until she gets new tires on it.

5.   Kimberley discovered an injured cat; she saw that it had a bleeding paw.

EXERCISE 2.1.2

Identify the pronouns in the following sentences and state the noun each one replaces.

1. Nita and Jamie carried their books.

2. The dog chased its tail; the male cat licked his paws.

3. After the rain had stopped, the sky returned to its natural colour. Then the men drove off in their cars.

4. John owns a bungalow and it is beautiful.

5. Whose coat is on the chair—Arpita's or Lily's?

EXERCISE 2.1.3

Each underlined pronoun in the following sentences refers to a particular word in that sentence. Draw an arrow from the underlined pronoun to the word to which it refers.

■ **Example:**

The man must remember to buy his ticket.

1. Each of the girls is excited about her dance recital.

2. I thought I had the key to the house; however, when we got home, I could not find it in my purse.

3. Intermediate players must learn to compete against themselves.

4. Some of the classes I teach are small because students are not required to take them.

5. Before approaching a strange animal, one should make sure it is not rabid.

2.2 COMMON ERRORS—THE CORRECT USE OF PRONOUNS

An **antecedent** is a word to which a pronoun refers back, as in this example:

Uncle Ted raises chickens. *He* keeps *them* in cages in the backyard.

In this sentence, the antecedent for *he* is the noun *Uncle Ted*. Which noun is the antecedent of the pronoun *them*? (The antecedent precedes or goes before the pronoun, replacing it.)

Like nouns, pronouns can be either singular or plural; therefore, always check to make sure the pronouns match or agree in number, gender, and person (first, second, or third person) with their antecedents. Remember two simple rules:

a) If the antecedent is singular, use a singular pronoun.

My *friend* jumped over the fence when *she* saw the bull.

She refers back to the antecedent *friend*. Since *friend* is singular, the pronoun that refers back to it (*she*) must also be singular.

b) If the antecedent is plural, use a plural pronoun.

My *friends* jumped over the fence when *they* saw the bull.

They refers back to the antecedent *friends*. Since *friends* is plural, the pronoun that refers back to it (*they*) must also be plural.

GENDER STEREOTYPES

While modern society promotes the equality of women and men, singular pronouns such as *he* and *she* in English are still gender specific. If a pronoun refers to a specific gender, then the appropriate gender must be used.

■ **Example:**

Every girl on the baseball team must pay her fee now.

The easiest way to avoid using a gender-specific pronoun is to use a plural noun as its antecedent (the noun to which it refers).

■ **Example:**

Players on the baseball team must pay their fees now.

Players is plural since it refers to more than one person; therefore, it is replaced by the plural pronoun *their*.

Consider the following gender-specific examples and how they could be rewritten to eliminate their gender bias.

1. A lawyer must pass his bar exams.

This sentence implies that all lawyers are male and this is not true. If you change the singular "lawyer" to the plural "lawyers," you are inclusive of both genders, and the pronoun "his" becomes the neutral "their."

Lawyers must pass their bar exams.

2. The sales*lady* showed me a radio.

The gender of the person showing me the radio has nothing to do with my decision.

The salesperson showed me a radio.

3. I did not like my grade; therefore, I appealed to the *chairman* of my department.

Employment equity and the recognition of the equality of men and women has made terms like *chairman* and *policeman* obsolete. These terms can be gender-neutral; for example, *police officer*.

I did not like my grade; therefore, I appealed to the chair of my department.

EXERCISE 2.2.1

Fill in the blanks in the following sentences, using *he*, *she*, *his*, *her*, *they*, *their*, or *them*. Draw an arrow from the pronoun to its antecedent. Avoid sexist language.

■ **Example:**

When Todd left, <u>he</u> hooked the latch carefully.

1. Sergio lost _____ cap at the hockey game.

2. The women told the policewoman that _____ were not guilty.

3. If students are sick, _____ should have a doctor's note.

4. Did the boys from Toronto bring _____ ballet slippers?

5. The officers told the soldiers that _____ must obey _____.

EXERCISE 2.2.2

Each of the underlined pronouns in the following sentences refers to a particular word in that sentence. Change any underlined pronoun that does not agree with the word to which it refers, and then rewrite the sentence correctly. If the word is already correct, write *C* beside the sentence.

Example: I thought Tira looked very elegant in <u>their</u> dress.
Corrected: I thought Tira looked very elegant in *her* dress.

1. When a person sees someone stealing a car, <u>they</u> should call the police right away.

   _____

2. The boys were careful to play safely with <u>their</u> toys.

   _____

3. A child must learn to take good care of <u>their</u> toys.

   _____

4. The Tragically Hip was ready to perform <u>its</u> newly recorded song.

   _____

5. A police officer must take many risks with <u>their</u> lives.

   _____

2.3   PERSON—SINGULAR AND PLURAL

Here is a list of common pronouns.

	Singular	**Plural**
1st person	I, me, my	we, us, our
2nd person	you, your	you, your
3rd person	he, him, his she, her, hers it, it, its	they, them, their

NOTE: Its is the possessive form of *it*, and does not require an apostrophe ('). None of the possessive pronouns requires an apostrophe. If the apostrophe were inserted (*it's*), it would be a contraction of *it is*. Contractions are not considered acceptable in formal English writing.

NOTE: You and *your* may be either singular or plural.

When we refer to the person of a pronoun, we are referring to the relationship of the writer, (or speaker) to the pronoun. If you want your readers to focus on you, then use the **first person** (*I*). If you want them to focus on how the subject directly relates to them, then use the **second person** (*you*). If you want your readers to focus on the subject, then use the **third person** (*he*, *she*, *it*).

First Person: I, we

Pronouns of the first person refer to the person who is speaking or writing.

> *I* have marked all the essays.

The focus of this sentence is on *I*.

Second Person: you

Pronouns of the second person refer to the person being spoken to.

> *Your* essay has been marked.

Third Person: he, she, it, they

Pronouns of the third person refer to the person or thing spoken about. This is also true for any noun or pronoun that may substitute for these persons or things.

> *His* essay has been marked.

2.4   KINDS (CLASSES) OF PRONOUNS

There are several kinds or classes of pronouns. **Personal pronouns** stand for persons. **Possessive pronouns** are used to show possession or ownership. **Demonstrative pronouns** point out a particular person or thing. **Relative pronouns** are used to introduce dependent adjective clauses. **Interrogative pronouns** are used in asking questions. **Indefinite pronouns** are those that stand for no particular person or thing. **Reflexive pronouns** indicate that someone did something to himself or herself, and include those ending in *-self* and *-selves.*

Personal: I, you, he, she it, we, they, me, us, him, her, his, hers, us
> *She* sold what *she* owned to *us.*

Possessive: my, mine, ours, your, yours, her, his, her, its, theirs, their
> I have *my* books. Please leave *hers* (or *his*) on the desk.

Demonstrative: this, that, these, those
> *This* is for you.

Relative: who, whoever, whom, whomever, whose, which, that
> Give this to *whomever* you choose.

Interrogative: who?, whom?, which?, whose?, what?
> *Whose* is this?

Indefinite: All the pronouns that end with *-one, -thing,* and *-body,* such as *anybody, anyone, anything, everybody, everything, everyone, someone, something,* and *somebody* are included in this group. A number of other indefinite pronouns, such as *each, either, neither,* and *none,* are always singular in number and are followed by singular verbs (see Module 3).
> *Everyone* must remove *his* or *her* shoes.

> **NOTE:** These pronouns are *always* singular in number. Some indefinite pronouns, however, are plural: *few, many, most, several, some.* These, of course, should be followed by plural verbs.

Reflexive: All the pronouns that end with *-self* or *-selves,* such as *myself, yourself, himself, herself, itself, ourselves, yourselves,* and *themselves,* are never used alone and must come after the words to which they refer as in the following example:
> We bought *ourselves* a cabin cruiser.

EXERCISE 2.4.1

In the following sentences, underline the correct pronoun in parentheses. Draw an arrow to the word to which the pronoun refers.

■ **Example:**

The children brought (his, <u>their</u>) lunches to school.

Their modifies the noun *lunches*.

1. I bought a new dress, and (it, they) looks beautiful.

2. He bought a pair of pants, but (it, they) had to be returned because (it, they) were too small.

3. If everyone does (his, their) best, (he, they) will succeed.

4. The toddler insisted on doing it (himself, themselves).

5. A good chiropractor knows how to do (his, their) job well.

2.5   PRONOUN NUMBER

The **number** of a pronoun refers to whether it is *singular* or *plural*. A singular pronoun refers to a single person, place, or thing, whereas a plural pronoun refers to more than one person, place, or thing.

	Singular	**Plural**
1st person	I, me, my	we, us, our, ours
2nd person	you, your, yours	you, your, yours
3rd person	he, she, it his, her, hers, its him, her, it	they their, theirs them
	whomever, who	whoever, whose, whom who, whose, whom

2.6   PRONOUN CASE

As already mentioned in Module 1, there are three cases in the English language: **subjective**, **possessive**, and **objective**. A pronoun is *subjective* case when it is used as a subject or as the complement of a linking verb (see Module 3). Pronouns denoting *possession* are shown on the following page. Observe that they change their forms depending on who is doing the possessing. The *objective* form of a pronoun is used for objects of verbs or objects of prepositions.

	Personal	**Relative**
Subjective	I, you, he, she, it, we, they	who, which, that
Possessive	mine, yours, his, hers, its, our, ours, their, theirs	whose
Objective	me, you, him, her, it, us them	whom, what, that

To decide which pronoun is correct, you should complete the sentence to see if it makes sense.

> He likes her more than I *(like her)*.

> He likes her more than *(he likes)* me.

This will help you avoid common errors with pronouns.

PRONOUNS THAT FUNCTION AS ADJECTIVES

While adjectives—words that modify nouns—will be discussed in Module 4, you should know about this special use of pronouns. Possessive pronouns can be used as adjectives to refer to nouns and to show possession.

■ **Examples:**

> Natsuno put on *her* shoes.

Her is a pronoun functioning as an adjective because it modifies the noun *shoes*. The antecedent is *Natsuno*; *her* describes the specific shoes that belong to Natsuno.

> The puppy chased *its* tail around and around in circles until it was dizzy.

Its functions as an adjective modifying the noun, *tail*.

> **NOTE:** *Its* is spelled without an apostrophe.

In the above examples, the words are used as adjectives describing nouns. They are pronouns in form and each takes the place of a noun.

RELATIVE PRONOUNS: *WHO, WHOEVER, WHOM, WHOMEVER*

Who and *whoever* are in the subjective case. *Whom* and *whomever* are in the objective case. They are always used to refer to people. *That* and *which* refer to everything else.

■ **Examples:**

> The young girl who was hurt climbing the tree is in the hospital.

> The man who was present during the ceremony appeared nervous.

The raccoon that I saw looked rabid.

The woman whom the president chose for the job was excited.

Whoever wishes may leave now.

Tell whomever you wish.

It is difficult to decide when to use *who* or *whom*. Keep this rule in mind: *who* is always used for subjective case and *whom* is used for objective case (see section 1.5).

EXERCISE 2.6.1

Underline the appropriate case in the following, then rewrite the sentence correctly:

1. When (us, we, our) decided to go on the trip, (us, we, our) children were not very happy.

   _____

2. To (who, whom) should (me, I) address this letter?

   _____

3. Yuri and (me, I) were angry at (mine, my, me) cat for scaring the bird.

   _____

4. (Who, Whose, Whom) books are (they, them, these)?

   _____

5. (Your, You're, You) are not going to see (she, hers, her) again. Do (your, you, they) understand me?

   _____

EXERCISE 2.6.2

In the following sentences underline the pronouns and state the person, number, kind, and case of each.

■ **Example:**

We were never sure *who* was the criminal in this case. Did *everyone* suffer for the damage Fred caused?

Pronoun	Kind	Case	Relation
we	1st person plural personal pronoun	subjective	subject of the verb *were*
who	3rd person singular relative pronoun	subjective	subject of the verb *was*
everyone	3rd person singular indefinite pronoun	subjective	subject of the verb *did suffer*

NOTE: The number of pronouns is indicated in parentheses at the end of each sentence.

1. About whom was he talking? (2)

   _____

2. Whoever can jump that distance will get her gold medal. (3)

   _____

3. Simone and I went to our friend's lecture in Toronto, where we once lived. (3)

   _____

4. For him and me there will be no chance of escaping it. (3)

   _____

5. Several of these books are no longer published. (2)

   _____

EXERCISE 2.6.3

Rewrite the following sentences, correcting the pronouns where necessary. Explain your corrections. If a sentence is already correct, explain why the pronoun is right.

1. Is this the cat who ate the mouse?

   _____

2. The road that I took led me past some of the most beautiful homes that me had ever seen.

   _____

3. The store that we entered was owned by a little old lady that was very frail looking.

   _____

4. The office feels cozy to everyone who walks through the door.

   _____

5. Anyone that had not done their homework would get the jitters.

   _____

ANSWER KEY

EXERCISE 2.1.1

1. Janine twisted an ankle while she was figure skating.
   she—Janine
3. "Mrs. Kwak told us to wait until she came back," replied the girls.
   us—girls; she—Mrs. Kwak
5. Kimberley discovered an injured cat; she saw that it had a bleeding paw.
   she—Kimberley; it—cat

EXERCISE 2.1.2

1. their; Nita and Jamie
3. its, sky; their, men
5. whose, Arpita's or Lily's

EXERCISE 2.1.3

1. Each of the girls is excited about her dance recital.
3. Intermediate players must learn to compete against themselves.
5. Before approaching a strange animal, one should make sure it is not rabid.

EXERCISE 2.2.1

1. Sergio lost his cap at the hockey game.
3. If students are sick, they should have a doctor's note.
5. The officers told the soldiers that they must obey them.

EXERCISE 2.2.2

1. When a person sees someone stealing a car, he (or she) should call the police right away.
3. A child must learn to take good care of his (or her) toys.
5. A police officer must take many risks with his (or her) life.

EXERCISE 2.4.1

1. I bought a new dress, and it looks beautiful.
3. If everyone does his (or her) best, he (or she) will succeed.
5. A good chiropractor knows how to do his (or her) job well.
   His modifies the noun job.

EXERCISE 2.6.1

1. When we decided to go on the trip, our children were not very happy.
3. Yuri and I were angry at my cat for scaring the bird.
5. You are not going to see her again. Do you understand me?

EXERCISE 2.6.2

	Pronoun	**Kind**	**Case**	**Relation**
1.	whom	3rd person interrogative	objective	subject of verb *was*
	he	3rd person subjective	subjective	object of verb *talking*
3.	I	1st person personal	subjective	subject of the sentence
	our	1st person possessive	possessive	modifies noun *friend*
	we	1st person plural personal	personal	subject of subordinate clause
5.	several	3rd person indefinite	subjective	subject of the sentence
	these	3rd person demonstrative	objective	modifies the noun *books*

EXERCISE 2.6.3

1. Is this the cat *that* ate the mouse?
   Who refers only to persons.
3. The store that we entered was owned by a little old lady *who* was very frail looking.
   That refers to things; *who* refers to persons.
5. Anyone *who* had not done *his* (or *her*) homework would get the jitters.
   Who is required because it relates back to a person (*anyone*).
   His (or *her*) is required to agree in number with its antecedent *anyone*.

MODULE 3

VERBS

Learning Outcome Statement

By becoming familiar with the different tenses, moods, and voices of verbs, and by successfully completing a series of module exercises, you will be able to use verbs in sentences.

VERBS

Where would we be without verbs? We would simply have a number of persons, places, things, and ideas (nouns), or their substitutes (pronouns) sitting around with no place to go, nothing to do, and no sense of time.

Most verbs tell us what action is taking place; in other words, what the subject or main noun of the sentence is doing. This action may be visible, such as *run*, *sleep*, *talk*, or hidden and abstract, such as *think*, *wonder*, or *understand*. Some verbs may also describe what we call the "state of being" of the subject, as in "He is happy" or "She is tired." Whatever kind of verb we have, no sentence is complete without one, since a sentence must have both a subject, or noun, and a predicate, or verb. Let us first examine the three basic types of verbs.

3.1 CATEGORIES OF VERBS

Verbs fall into one of three categories:

1. **transitive**, requiring an object;
2. **intransitive**, having no object;
3. **linking**, taking a subjective completion (or complement of the subject; see nouns as complements in Module 1).

TRANSITIVE VERBS

Start looking for the object of the verb by asking the verb questions: *whom?* for persons *what?* for things (see Module 1). One of the jobs of a noun (or one of its substitutes; for example, pronouns, noun phrases, or noun clauses) is to work as the object of a verb. To understand exactly what this means, look at the following examples:

1. Sadian *likes* (what?) cookies.

2. Marguerite *plays* (what?) the piano.

3. Leena *loves* (whom?) her son.

All of the verbs in the above examples are transitive because they all have objects—a thing (or things) that receives the action in order to complete the idea. The word "transitive" comes from the Latin root *trans-*, meaning "across" (as in *transportation* or *transfer*). The transitive verb therefore must move the action of the subject across to an object.

INTRANSITIVE VERBS

This kind of verb does *not* transfer action to an object, simply because the statement is complete without an object. The action expressed by an intransitive verb is self-contained. Intransitive verbs may be modified by adverbs or have no modifiers at all.

■ **Examples:**

1. The firecrackers exploded.

2. The audience applauded.

Neither of these sentences has an object following the verb; both verbs are intransitive.

> 3. The firecrackers exploded *with a bang.*

> 4. The audience applauded *loudly.*

These two sentences both have adverbial modifiers—*with a bang* and *loudly*—following their verbs. However, they still have no objects. Consequently, both verbs are still intransitive. (See Module 4 for information regarding adverbs.)

LINKING VERBS

Linking verbs "link" the subject of the sentence with another word. They describe the "state of being" of the subject. If we wish to add to the picture of the subject in the mind of our reader, we might say something like:

> 1. Newfoundland is very *scenic.* (adjective)

> 2. Newfoundland is Canada's most *eastern province.* (noun)

We wish to connect *Newfoundland* and *scenic* or *Newfoundland* and *eastern province*. We wish to complete the image of the subject of the sentence, *Newfoundland*.

> 3. The CN Tower is very *tall.* (adjective)

> 4. The CN Tower is the world's tallest free-standing *structure.* (noun)

In both examples, we are linking the CN Tower to an additional image, connecting the two word groups, and identifying them with each other. To what is the CN Tower linked?

> **NOTE:** No action is involved in these groups of verbs.

In the first example, the subjective completion, the thing that completes the image of the subject of the sentence, is an adjective (see Module 4). In the second, it is a noun. Both identify the verb as a linking verb. If a linking verb is followed by a pronoun, we would use the subjective case of the pronoun, as in "Do not worry; it is I."

> **NOTE:** When a linking verb is completed by a noun or pronoun, the noun or pronoun will be the same thing as the subject noun or pronoun. When a linking verb is completed by an adjective, the adjective will modify the subject.

The most common linking verbs are *is*, *are*, *was*, and *were* (forms of the verb *to be*). Some others are *seem*, *taste*, *appear*, and *become*. Notice that these all relate to something sensory about a subject—something dealing with the five senses.

Do not confuse linking verbs with **helping** verbs. Helping verbs help create a time sense when used with the main verb, such as *is running*. Here the helper verb *is* is used with the main verb, *running*. For example:

The deer is *running* through the woods.

EXERCISE 3.1.1

Identify which of the following sentences have linking verbs. In a sentence, identify their subjective completions. One of these sentences contains an intransitive verb.

1. After taking a walk last night, I felt cold.

2. Judy and her dog ran in circles.

3. She was the chair of Ontario Hydro last year.

4. The whole affair appeared hopeless.

5. John A. Macdonald was a leader.

NOTE: The presence or absence of a modifying word or words does not change an action. The phrases merely describe when, where, why, or how the action took place. They tell us nothing about the subject, and, therefore, should not be confused with subjective completions, which are adjectives or nouns.

To help clarify this, look at the following examples:

He *breathed* the fresh air.

The verb *breathed* is transitive since it has the noun object *air*.

He *breathed* slowly.

The verb *breathed* in this example is intransitive. *Slowly* is an adverb (see Module 4) describing the breathing, but it is not a noun object.

The dog *smells* the food.

The verb *smells* is the transitive form of the verb *to smell*; its object is *the food*.

The dog *smells* badly.

The verb *smells* is intransitive. It has no object, but is followed by the adverb *badly,* which describes it.

EXERCISE 3.1.2

Do the following sentences use intransitive or transitive verbs? In a sentence or two, explain your answers.

1. We went over to the delicatessen to buy some bagels.

2. The quarterback grabbed the ball and ran to his right.

_____

_____

3. Janet dragged the canoe out of the water.

_____

_____

4. He fell off the horse and broke his neck.

_____

_____

5. The seagull flew high in the air.

_____

_____

EXERCISE 3.1.3

In a sentence, indicate (1) which verbs are transitive and identify their object; (2) which verbs are intransitive; and (3) which verbs are linking, and identify their subjective completion.

1. We went to the park to play baseball.

_____

_____

2. The couple seems happy.

_____

_____

3. I waited for the bus impatiently.

_____

_____

4. I gave the card to you.

_____

_____

5. Nothing seems the same any more.

3.2 ACTIVE AND PASSIVE VOICE

If the subject performs the action of the verb, the verb is said to be in the **active voice**. If the subject does not perform the action of the verb, the verb is said to be in the **passive voice**.

In the active voice, the subject is performing the action of the verb. In the passive voice, the subject is having something done to it by the object of the preposition *by*, which may be stated or only understood.

■ Examples:

    1. Farahnaz watched the hockey game.

    2. The hockey game was watched *by* Farahnaz.

In the first example Farahnaz is doing the watching (the action). She is doing something to the object (*game*). Note also that the action flows forward from the subject (*Farahnaz*), through the verb (*watched*) to the object (*game*).

In the second example the game is not doing the watching. Instead, the action flows backward from the object of the preposition (*by*), through the verb (*was watched*), to the subject (*game*).

Although the passive voice may seem awkward, there are times when it is appropriate. For example, if you are writing to a customer who has damaged an item beyond repair, you might say, "You have broken this item beyond repair." Since this sounds like an insult, you risk losing that person as a customer; you should write, "This item has been broken beyond repair," tactfully omitting the implied "by you."

How does one recognize the passive voice, apart from recognizing that the subject is not doing the action of the verb? The passive voice always contains some form of the verb *to be*, plus the past participle of the main verb. The word *by* is either present or understood. For example:

Programs *were* hand*ed* out *by* the ushers.

Programs *were* hand*ed* out.

Both of these sentences contain a form of the verb *to be* (*were*), plus a past participle (*handed*). The preposition *by* is also present. In the first example, it is actually stated; in the second, it is merely implied or understood, by the reader. Here are more examples:

The basement *was* flood*ed by* heavy rains. (passive)

The basement *was* flood*ed.* (passive)

Cookies *are* lik*ed by* Shayamal. (passive)

Shayamal likes cookies. (active)

The piano *is* play*ed by* Meg. (passive)

Meg plays the piano. (active)

Her son *is* lov*ed by* Anna (passive)

Anna loves her son. (active)

Since the active voice is generally preferred, it is the voice most used in English. *A word of caution:* Do not change voice within a sentence. Use the active only, or the passive only. Changing from active to passive within a sentence tends to impede its forward flow.

EXERCISE 3.2.1

Underline the verbs in the following sentences, and state whether they are in the active or passive voice.

1. I am going to the circus. _____

2. What is being done to correct the problem? _____

3. The floods receded slowly. _____

4. Has anyone finished the test yet? _____

5. I shall endeavour to rectify the situation. _____

EXERCISE 3.2.2

Rewrite the following sentences, changing all active voice verbs to passive, and all passive voice verbs to active. When you make the changes, keep the same tense.

1. He is changing his bicycle tire.

_____

2. *Hamlet* was read by the teacher.

_____

3. The rules for the examination were stated clearly.

_____

4. *Lawrence of Arabia* is considered to be a classic film.

_____

5. Sheila is answering her mother's call.

_____

3.3 MOOD OF A VERB

Verbs come in three different moods: *indicative*, *imperative*, and *subjunctive*. The mood of the verb indicates something about the meaning of the sentence.

INDICATIVE MOOD

This mood is used to make a simple statement or to ask a question. It is a matter-of-fact kind of mood and can be found in any tense.

■ **Example:**

> The man walked/is walking/walks home.

IMPERATIVE MOOD

Use the imperative mood to issue commands, orders, or strong requests. Notice that "Go home," has no obvious actor in it. Who is the person who will do the action of "going"? The assumed subject in this sentence is *you*. You are the person who will *go*. The *you* is understood to be the subject of the sentence: "(You) go home."

SUBJUNCTIVE MOOD

This is a little tougher to understand. It is used to express a wish or to describe a condition that is not true or real.

■ **Examples:**

> I wish I *were* a wealthy person. (Not true; you are not a wealthy person.)
>
> If she *were* younger, she would not be so wise.

> *NOTE:* The three singular persons (I, you, he/she/it) and all nouns will use the *were* form of the verb *to be* in the subjunctive mood. This mood also tends to be rather formal and is used to express determination, or to give a command that is not written in the imperative format.

■ **Examples:**

> I insist that he *conform* to the dress code.
>
> The general ordered that all troops *be* in dress uniform.

EXERCISE 3.3.1

Identify the mood of the verbs in the following sentences. Then write a sentence to explain your answer.

1. We hoped we would win Lotto 649.

   mood:_____

   _____

   _____

2. Don't you come in here!

   mood: _____

   _____

   _____

3. The dog chewed up my slipper!

   mood: _____

   _____

   _____

4. Martin insisted he had not taken the money.

   mood: _____

   _____

   _____

5. Long may our queen reign.

   mood: _____

   _____

   _____

3.4   FORMS OF A VERB

All verb tenses are built on three forms: **present**, **past**, and **past participle**. These are known as the principal parts of the verb.

PRESENT

This first principal part is used to form the present tense; for example, *I go* or *she works*. You can think of this as the base form of the verb. In this form, you are generally using the verb to show one of the following:

   1. a present action: They *are* busy.

   2. a general truth: Babies *cry*.

   3. a habitual action: Chandra-Li *drinks* coffee in the morning.

PAST

The second principal part is used to form the past tenses, according to the following rules:

1. If the present tense ends in *e*, add *-d* (*save, saved*).

2. If the present tense does not end in *e*, add *ed* (*walk, walked*).

3. If the present tense ends in *y*, change the *y* to *i* and add *-ed* (*hurry, hurried*).

4. If the present tense has only a single vowel and ends in a single consonant, repeat the last consonant and add *-ed* (*drop, dropped*).

PAST PARTICIPLE

For regular verbs, this third principal part has exactly the same form as the past and is used with helper verbs to form the perfect tenses. (See "Verb Tenses," below, and Module 5.)

Irregular Verb Chart—Principal Parts

Remember that most English verbs, known as "regular" verbs, form their past and past participles by adding *-ed* to their present tense. All other verbs are called "irregular." Below is a chart of some of the more common irregular verbs (those that do not form their past tense and past participles by adding *-ed* to the present tense). The three forms below are known as the principal parts of the verb.

Present	**Past**	**Past Participle** (Used with the helper verbs *have* and *had*)
bear	bore	borne
begin	began	begun
bit	bit	bitten
blow	blew	blown
break	broke	broken
bring	brought	brought
burst *	burst *	burst *
build	built	built
buy	bought	bought
catch	caught	caught
choose	chose	chosen
come	came	come
cut *	cut *	cut *
dive	dived (*or* dove)	dived
do	did	done
draw	drew	drawn

Present	**Past**	**Past Participle** (Used with the helper verbs *have* and *had*)
drink	drank	drunk
drive	drove	driven
eat	ate	eaten
fall	fell	fallen
feed	fed	fed
find	found	found
fling	flung	flung
fly	flew	flown
forget	forgot	forgotten
freeze	froze	frozen
get	got	got
give	gave	given
go	went	gone
hang (*persons*)	hanged	hanged
hang (*things*)	hung	hung
hit *	hit *	hit *
hurt *	hurt *	hurt *
know	knew	known
lay	laid	laid (*to put, to place*)
lie (*persons*)	lay	lain (*to be supine*)
lie	lied	lied (*to tell an untruth*)
lead	led	led
lend	lent	lent
read *	read *	read *
ride	rode	ridden
ring	rang	rung
rise	rise	risen
say	said	said
see	saw	seen
set *	set *	set *
sit	sat	sat
shake	shook	shaken
shrink	shrank	shrunk
shine	shone	shone
sink	sank	sunk
spring	sprang	sprung

continued

Present	Past	Past Participle (Used with the helper verbs *have* and *had*)
steal	stole	stolen
swim	swam	swum
take	took	taken
tear	tore	torn
throw	threw	thrown
write	wrote	written

NOTE: All three principal parts of the verbs marked with an asterisk * are the same, and have the same pronunciation, with one exception. The present form of *read* is pronounced "reed"; the past and past participle is pronounced "red."

EXERCISE 3.4.1

Write sentences using the following verbs in the forms requested in parentheses.

1. fly   (past participle) _____

_____

2. run   (past) _____

_____

3. eaten (past) _____

_____

4. study (past) _____

_____

5. be   (past)_____

_____

3.5   VERB TENSES

The best way to understand tenses is to remember the following: tenses give us a "time sense" of the action of the verb. Tenses tell us exactly when an action happened without having to provide a detailed wordy description.

SIMPLE TENSES

There are essentially three points in time we care about: then, now, and to come. In order to get a clearer idea of verb tenses, picture yourself on a time line going from the past, through the present, and into the future.

Past	Present	Future
studied	study	will study
asked	ask	will ask
laughed	laugh	will laugh
ran	run	will run

These represent the **three simple tenses**. Look at the chart below for the regular verb *to play* and the irregular verb *to do*.

Simple Past	Simple Present	Simple Future
(using past form)	(using present form)	(using "will" + present form)
played	play	shall play (or) will play
did	do	shall do (or) will do

The simple tense is called "simple" because it represents the simplest, or easiest, way a verb can be expressed in either the past, the present, or the future.

Shall is used as a helping verb in the first person only. *Will* is used as a helping verb in the second and third persons.

PROGRESSIVE TENSES

Our lives are not quite that "simple"; therefore, we require some additional help in accurately depicting at which point on our time line an event actually occurred. Say the action was continuous, and took place *over a period of time*, in the past, present, or the future. This means that the action would *progress* through a given time period. We would then use the progressive tense. To form the **progressive tense**, use past, present, and future forms of helping verbs plus the present participle (main verbs ending in *-ing*).

Past Progressive	Present Progressive	Future Progressive
was playing	am playing	will be playing
was doing	am doing	will be doing

Notice that we have used the past, present, and future tenses of the verb *be* plus the present participle of the verbs *play (playing)* and *do (doing)* in order to form the progressive tenses.

PERFECT TENSES

What if we wanted to describe something that happened *before* something else? Say we were talking about a week ago, but wanted to describe an action that took place before that. Or what if we wanted to discuss something that had not happened yet, but will have happened two days from now? For this situation, we make use of the **perfect tense**. "Perfect" in this sense, really means "complete" at some point in the past or future.

To form the perfect tense use the past and present form of helping verbs plus the past participle of the main verb:

Past Perfect	Present Perfect	Future Perfect
had played	have played	will have played
had done	have done	will have done

NOTE: Remember to use *shall* in the first person and *will* in the second and third persons for the future tenses.

PERFECT PROGRESSIVE TENSES

Say the action being discussed started at some point before our point on the time line, and then continued (progressed). In this case, we use the **perfect progressive**.

To form the perfect progressive, use the past *(had)* and present *(have)* forms of helping verbs, plus a form of the verb *be*, plus the present participle (-*ing* ending) of the main verb.

Past Perfect Progressive	Present Perfect Progressive	Future Perfect Progressive
had been playing	have been playing	shall/will have been playing
had been doing	have been doing	shall/will have been doing

Put another way: with the verb *had been playing*, *had been* is what makes this verb past perfect (*had* plus the past participle of the verb *be*); and the -*ing* of *playing* makes the whole verb past perfect progressive.

Here is another example:

	Past	Present	Future
Simple	worked was/were	work am/is	shall/will work will be
Progressive	was working was being	am working am being	shall/will be working shall/will be being
Perfect	had worked had been	have worked have been	shall/will have worked shall/will have been

Perfect Progressive	had been
	  working
		have been
		  working
			shall/will have been
			  working

Remember your time line. Your goal is to allow your readers to position themselves at exactly the same point in time at which you (the writer or speaker) have positioned yourself.

NOTE: Do not change tenses (from present to past, or past to present) within a sentence.

EMPHATIC TENSE

The helping verbs in this tense are used for emphasis or promise.

Past	Present	Future
did work	do work	will work (1st person)
		shall work (2nd person)
		shall work (3rd person)
did do	do do	will (or shall) do

Note that the helping verb for denoting the **past emphatic** tense is *did*, and the helping verb for denoting the **present emphatic** is *do*. Note also that the **future emphatic** is formed by reversing the helping verbs *shall* and *will*.

■ **Examples:**

I *did* work last night. (past emphatic)

I *do* work diligently every day. (present emphatic)

I *will* work hard, never fear. (future emphatic)

I *did* do what you told me. (past emphatic)

I *do* do my homework every day. (present emphatic)

I *will* do whatever you ask. (future emphatic)

EXERCISE 3.5.1

The future emphatic here shows determination or expresses a promise.

In the following sentences, name the tenses of the given verbs as simple or emphatic (past, present, or future), and give reasons for your answers.

1. You shall do the assignment, or else!

tense:

_____

reason:

_____

_____

2. She will cook supper when she comes home.

   tense:

   _____

   reason:

   _____

   _____

3. Shall we go to a movie this evening?

   tense:

   _____

   reason:

   _____

   _____

4. I will be at the meeting, I promise you.

   tense:

   _____

   reason:

   _____

   _____

5. Did he speak to you about the fire?

   tense:

   _____

   reason:

   _____

   _____

EXERCISE 3.5.2

Write the three principal parts of the following verbs:

1. scream   _____

2. jump   _____

3. copy   _____

4. think   _____

5. see   _____

EXERCISE 3.5.3

In the blank provided, write the correct form of the irregular verb given in parentheses.

■ **Example:**

Last year John _____ won _____ the salesmanship award. (win)

1. Yesterday she _____ the report to Mr. Domville. (bring)

2. The tree had _____ over onto the car. (blow)

3. The meeting has already _____ . (begin)

4. The editor has _____ several pages from the manuscript. (cut)

5. Ms. Jones had _____ tired of her new job. (grow)

EXERCISE 3.5.4

Write sentences in which you use the following verbs in the specified tense:

1. *fly* in the present perfect

_____

2. *run* in the progressive future

_____

3. *eat* in the future perfect

_____

4. *study* in the simple past

_____

5. *be* in the present perfect

_____

3.6 COMMON ERROR—SUBJECT AND VERB AGREEMENT

When we speak of agreement of subject and verb, we are talking in terms of *agreement in number*. In other words, if the bare subject is singular, the verb should be in the correct form to agree with that number; the same is true of plurals.

When we develop the forms of all tenses of verbs, we use a simple chart like the one that follows, which shows the present tense of the verb *to walk.*

	Singular	Plural
First Person	I walk	we walk
Second Person	you walk	you walk
Third Person	he/she/it walks	they walk

The first person involves you (singular) and any group in which you are included (plural); the second person involves the person (singular) or persons (plural) to whom you are speaking; and the third person involves another person or persons about whom you and your audience are speaking. Note carefully that we have added an *s* (*walks*) for the third person singular.

> *NOTE:* You may have difficulty with the third person singular verb ending. You may assume that because it ends with *s*, it must be plural. This is not necessarily true.

The vast majority of verbs are **regular**. They form their second and third principal parts by adding *-ed* as endings, for example, *walk, walked, walked*.

Irregular verbs change their form and spelling throughout the persons (first, second, and third). Observe the present tense of the irregular verb *to be*:

	Singular	Plural
First Person	I am	we are
Second Person	you are	you are
Third Person	he/she/it is	they are

Whether the verb is regular or irregular, there will be some sort of change, usually in the third person singular.

In order to achieve agreement, it is essential that you are able to identify the subject of the sentence. This is relatively simple in the natural format of the sentence, in which the subject precedes the verb directly. But what happens when the subject is not at the beginning of the sentence?

Examine the following sentences.

> There are particles of sand in my shoe.

The bare subject, *particles*, is plural and agrees in number with the verb *are*. *There* is not a subject.

> A herd of elephants and giraffes runs on the plain.

The bare subject, *herd*, is singular and agrees with the singular verb *runs*.

> Elephants and giraffes run on the plain.

The subject is *elephants and giraffes*. Since there is more than one, the subject is plural and must agree with the plural verb, *run*.

Here are some other guidelines to help you determine which form to use:

1. *All* and *some* can be singular or plural depending on their meaning. For example:

> <u>All</u> of the students <u>are</u> gone.   *or*   <u>All</u> <u>is</u> finished.
>
> <u>Some</u> of the candies <u>are</u> left.   *or*   <u>Some</u> of the candy <u>is</u> left.

NOTE: The verb always agrees in number with the bare subject.

2. Units of time, money, and measure are considered singular subjects. For example:

    Six months <u>is</u> the time limit.

    One hundred dollars <u>is</u> the amount owed.

    Three-quarters of a tablespoon <u>is</u> all you require.

3. Subjects joined with *or* or *nor:*

    a) If both subjects are singular, they are treated the same as a singular subject.

    b) If one is singular and the other plural, the verb agrees with the nearer subject. For example:

    Neither the horse nor the cattle <u>go</u> to that field. (plural)

    Neither the cattle nor the horse <u>goes</u> to that field. (singular)

(See correlative conjunctions in Module 6.)

4. Indefinite pronouns (see Module 2) are almost always singular, and the verb must agree in number with such subjects. For example:

    None of the boys <u>is</u> coming.

EXERCISE 3.6.1

Rewrite the following sentences, using the correct form of the verb to agree with the subject. Explain your answer.

1. Most of the students (bring) their own lunch.

   _____

2. Many students (bring) their own lunch.

   _____

3. There (be) shredded paper all over the desk.

   _____

4. No one (ask) any questions.

   _____

5. Where (do) the birds go in winter?

   _____

ANSWER KEY

EXERCISE 3.1.1

1. *felt*—linking verb; *cold*—subjective completion
3. *was*—linking verb; *chairperson*—subjective completion
5. *is*—linking verb; *leader*—subjective completion

EXERCISE 3.1.2

1. *went*—intransitive
3. *dragged*—transitive; object—*canoe*
5. *flew*—intransitive

EXERCISE 3.1.3

1. *went*—intransitive verb
3. *waited*—intransitive verb
5. *seems*—linking verb; *same*—noun, subjective completion

EXERCISE 3.2.1

1. *am going*—active
3. *receded*—active
5. *shall endeavour*—active

EXERCISE 3.2.2

1. His bicycle tire is being changed by him.
3. (The professor) clearly stated the rules for the examination.
5. Her mother's call is being answered by Sheila.
The subjects in parentheses will vary.

EXERCISE 3.3.1

1. subjunctive
3. indicative
5. subjunctive
Explanations will vary.

EXERCISE 3.4.1

1. had flown
3. ate
5. was
Sentences will vary.

EXERCISE 3.5.1

1. *shall do*	future emphatic	(determination or promise)
3. *shall go*	simple future	(statement of fact)
5. *did speak*	past emphatic	(helping verb *did*)

EXERCISE 3.5.2

1 scream, screamed, screamed
3. copy, copied, copied
5. see, saw, seen

EXERCISE 3.5.3

    1 brought
    3. begun
    5. grown

EXERCISE 3.5.4

    1. have flown
    3. shall (will) have eaten
    5. have been
    Sentences will vary.

EXERCISE 3.6.1

    1. Most of the students bring their own lunch.
    3. There is shredded paper all over the desk.
    5. Where do the birds go in the winter?

MODULE

4

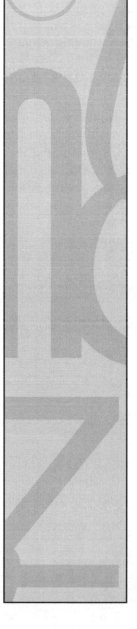

ADJECTIVES AND ADVERBS

Learning Outcome Statement

By successfully completing a series of module exercises, you will be able to correctly use the different types of adjectives and adverbs.

ADJECTIVES AND ADVERBS

Adjectives and adverbs provide interest in your writing by describing any qualities or characteristics of the words they modify. There are some easy ways to identify adjectives and adverbs. Ask yourself which words in the sentence describe other words.

Once you have identified the descriptive words, a few rules of thumb will be handy:

1. Adjectives modify only nouns or pronouns.

2. Adverbs modify verbs, verb forms, adjectives, and other adverbs, but not nouns or pronouns.

4.1 ADJECTIVES

A noun by itself is simply a person, place, thing, or idea. When nouns are described, they become more interesting and precise. **Adjectives** are words that make meaning clearer by describing, or *modifying*, nouns or pronouns. Modify means to change the meaning of something.

Compare the following sentences:

The wind blew the bushes.

The *strong* wind blew the bushes.

The description in the first sentence is not as clear as the description in the second sentence. The adjective *strong* in the second sentence describes the wind and helps you picture the scene more exactly. Adjectives are very useful words because they help us give a clear picture of the person, place, thing, or idea we are describing by modifying or restricting its meaning. They make writing more interesting by clarifying the nouns and specifying their unique qualities.

Adjectives answer one of several questions in relationship to the nouns they describe: What kind? How much/many? or Which one?

■ **Examples:**

1) It was impossible to find a seat on the crowded bus.

(What kind of bus?—the *crowded* bus)

2) Heinrich had two tickets to the theatre.

(How many tickets?—*two* tickets)

3) I want to buy that car.

(Which car?—*that* car)

EXERCISE 4.1.1

Underline the adjectives in the following sentences. Then write a sentence describing the relationship of the adjectives to their nouns.

1. The tall, bearded man walked down the crowded street.

_____

_____

2. The tired, old man walked down the deserted, dirty alley.

_____

_____

3. The tall, graceful model sauntered down the runway.

_____

_____

4. Mary's little sister is a good actress.

_____

_____

5. The large, dirty elephant rolled in the dirt.

_____

_____

EXERCISE 4.1.2

Write a sentence using adjectives to describe each of the following nouns:

1. night

_____

2. wind

_____

3. game

_____

4. battle

_____

5. water

_____

Adjectives do not always appear beside the noun or pronoun they modify. They can be separated from that noun or pronoun by a linking verb (see Module 3). For example:

Fred was happy.

The adjective *happy* modifies the subject noun *Fred*. The linking verb in the sentence is *was* since it links *Fred* with *happy*.

The most commonly used linking verbs are: *be, am, is, are, was, were, taste, smell, look, become, became, seem, feel, appear, sound*. These can be used to join a describing word to the noun or pronoun that it modifies.

EXERCISE 4.1.3

Select the adjective and draw an arrow to the noun they/it modify(ies). In a sentence, explain your decision.

■ **Example:**

Fred felt sad when he lost the race.

1. The sky looked gloomy before the storm.

   _____

2. The haunted house seemed strange.

   _____

3. The audience came alive at the performance.

   _____

4. They appeared lost in their new environment.

   _____

5. Shoshana felt sick after the race.

   _____

Some words can be used either as nouns or adjectives. The word *baseball* is usually a noun (see Module 1), but it can also be used as an adjective. For example:

Deiter received some tickets to the *baseball* game.

In this sentence, the word *baseball* modifies the noun *game*.

EXERCISE 4.1.4

Write sentences using the specified word as a noun, then as an adjective:

■ **Example:**

bus

The bus roared down the highway. (noun)

The bus tour was fun. (adjective)

1. gas

_____

_____

2. fire

_____

_____

3. gold

_____

_____

4. steel

_____

_____

5. winter

_____

_____

Adjectives can also be formed from proper nouns (see Module 1). When you use a proper noun as an adjective, you have to change its form. For example:

The Canadian flag is recognized worldwide.

Canadian is formed from the proper noun *Canada*. You write "the Canadian flag," not "the Canada flag," when identifying the flag that belongs to Canada. *Canadian* functions as an adjective because it modifies or describes the word *flag*.

EXERCISE 4.1.5

Make adjectives from the following proper nouns and use each in a sentence:

1. France   adjective: _____

_____

2. China   adjective: _____

_____

3. Norway   adjective: _____

4. America   adjective: _____

5. Spain   adjective: _____

Adjectives can also be formed from pronouns (see Module 2) that are used to indicate ownership or possession. These words look like pronouns, but they function as adjectives because they modify a noun. For example:

> *my* book, *his* pen, *that* car, *her* coat, *our* friend, *their* hats

EXERCISE 4.1.6

Underline the adjectives in each sentence. In a few sentences, state what each adjective modifies.

■ **Example:**

> Our big, black dog hid his beef bone under the ancient willow tree.

Adjectives: *Our*, *big*, and *black* modify the noun *dog*. *His* and *beef* modify the noun *bone*; *ancient* and *willow* modify the noun *tree*.

1. The two trained lions jumped through the large flaming hoop without burning their manes.

   _____

   _____

   _____

2. His dog has a wide, blunt head and a long, bushy tail.

   _____

   _____

   _____

3. For five hours, a thick fog covered the airport.

_____

_____

_____

4. Their summer clothes were in the other drawer.

_____

_____

_____

5. Irish settlers came to this huge country several years ago.

_____

_____

4.2   ARTICLES (THE, A, AN)

Articles are also adjectives. They modify nouns by making the noun either specific or general.

DEFINITE ARTICLES

The **definite article** _the_ is an adjective because it is used to modify nouns. It is called a definite article because it specifies a particular noun.

> _The_ woman came to our house.

> She knocked at _the_ door.

In these two examples, we are talking about a specific woman knocking at a particular door. The article _the_ makes the woman and the door specific.

INDEFINITE ARTICLES

Indefinite articles _a_ and _an_ are also adjectives because they modify nouns. But unlike the definite article, which specifies a particular thing, indefinite articles refer to members of groups.

> _A_ mechanic can repair _an_ automobile.

In this example, we are talking about one of many mechanics who can repair many different types of automobiles.

A boy entered *a* classroom. *The* boy asked for a book.

In this example, we are talking about one of many boys who entered one of many possible classrooms. If we were to continue talking about this particular boy, we would then switch to the definite article.

Be careful to use the correct indefinite articles. Use *a* before a word that begins with any one of the 21 consonants. Use *an* before a word that begins with a vowel (*a, e, i, o,* or *u*).

■ **Examples:**

a dog, a cat, an orange, an egg

DIFFERENCES BETWEEN DEFINITE AND INDEFINITE ARTICLES

There are three main differences between the definite and indefinite articles in English: these differences are related to number, specific degree, and the presence of noncountable nouns.

Number

An indefinite article can refer only to single nouns, such as *a picture*, or *an idea*. The definite article can refer to either singular or plural nouns, such as *the picture* or *the pictures*, *the idea* or *the ideas*. Your choice of articles will depend on the noun to which it is referring. Is it a specific picture or idea, or pictures and ideas in general?

Specific Degree

An indefinite article may classify a noun as belonging to a group, under which specific numbers of that group may be included:

You use *a* broom to sweep.

Brooms can have many different forms such as straw brooms or push brooms. The indefinite article means that you are referring to the whole class or group of possible brooms.

The definite article makes a noun specific:

You need to use *the* broom in the cupboard.

Here you are referring to a specific broom, the one in the cupboard. Since you are being specific, you need the definite article.

The Presence of Noncountable Nouns

An indefinite article cannot be used with nouns that are noncountable, such as *milk*, *water*, *salt*, *geography*; noncountable nouns do not signify a single unit. The definite article is used before a noncountable noun to restrict it or make it more specific.

Water is necessary to sustain life. (not restricted)

The water *in the fridge* is spring water. (restricted)

COUNTABLE OR NONCOUNTABLE NOUNS

While we are discussing articles, there are two types of nouns you should know about since they will help you select the appropriate articles. These are countable and noncountable nouns.

Countable nouns name things that can be counted. When you find the plural of a countable noun, you can think about dividing the group into its individual units. Consider the following:

box   This refers to a single unit.

boxes   This word is plural and it refers to a group, but the group is made up of individual units that can be counted.

A noncountable noun, as its name implies, is a thing that cannot be counted. Usually, noncountable nouns will be abstractions or things that cannot be cut up into single parts. Consider the following:

art

gasoline

cream

It is impossible to think of these as single units. They are also noncountable.

ARTICLES WITH SINGULAR, COUNTABLE NOUNS

You can use either a definite or an indefinite article with a singular, countable noun, such as *a* car and *the* car. Sometimes, an indefinite article means the same as *one*. For example:

They will be gone for *an* evening.

The definite article is used, for the most part, to make a noun more specific and has the same meaning as the demonstrative adjective *that* before a singular count-able noun (although *that* is more precise). For example:

Did you order *the* steak?

Did you order *that* steak?

You can also begin with an indefinite article to initially identify the object; then you can switch to the definite article. For example:

A letter came in the mail for you today. I put *the* letter on the table so that you would see it when you came home.

ARTICLES WITH PLURAL, COUNTABLE NOUNS

The indefinite article is never used with plurals. You can say *cars* or *the cars*. Instead of the indefinite article, you can use other adjectives:

I do not see *many* magazines on the rack.

Several parents were at the meeting.

The definite article *the* is used with plural, countable nouns to indicate a specific person or thing and is similar in meaning to the demonstrative adjective *that* (although *that* is more precise):

> Please hand me *the* hammer.

> *The* patient in the next bed was in a serious accident.

ARTICLES WITH NONCOUNTABLE NOUNS

The definite article is the only article that can be used to restrict a noun or make it more specific; the indefinite article is not able to do so. For example:

water, the water	Water was everywhere.
	The water in the ditch was muddy.
kindness, the kindness	Kindness is a virtue.
	The kindness she showed me I shall never forget.

> *NOTE:* Remember that the definite article with a noncountable noun limits or restricts it.

EXERCISE 4.2.1

Underline the correct article in parentheses, and explain your choice.

1. The judge was (a, an) serious person.

   _____

2. They threw (a, an) stone at me.

   _____

3. Did you have (a, an) egg for breakfast?

   _____

4. Mother put (a, an) orange in my lunchbox.

   _____

5. My teacher gave me (a, an) letter for my parents.

   _____

EXERCISE 4.2.2

Underline the adjectives in the following sentences. In a sentence, identify each adjective and explain which word each adjective modifies:

1. That kind of orange grows in the far south.

   _____

   _____

2. My mother and his aunt are good friends.

_____

_____

3. Most accidents can be avoided with a little caution.

_____

_____

4. Marco felt sad as he reeled in his line.

_____

_____

5. That skater is nimble.

_____

_____

4.3 COMPARATIVE ADJECTIVES

Adjectives can also be used to talk about the degree of things. When your coach tells you that you are a fast runner or skater, she is using the **positive** degree of the adjective *fast* to talk about you only. When talking about one person or thing, use the positive degree of comparison. *Faster* is the **comparative** degree of the adjective or adverb *fast*. When your coach says, "You are faster than Jane," she is comparing you to another person. When comparing two things, use the comparative degree. When forming the comparative degree, the ending *-er* is often added to the positive degree. *Fastest* is the **superlative** degree of the adjective *fast*. Here, your coach says, "You are the fastest runner on the team." She is comparing you to more than one person. Use the superlative degree of the adjective when comparing three or more things. When forming the superlative degree, the ending *-est* is usually added to the positive degree. For example:

> The coach said that John was a *fast* skater.

> He said Heinrich was *faster* than John, and Naidoo was the *fastest* of the three skaters.

The regular way to form the comparative and superlative of adjectives and adverbs of one syllable is by adding *-er* or *-est*, respectively. On multiple-syllable adjectives and adverbs, you will have to take extra care with your spelling.

To form the comparative and superlative of adjectives that end in *-y*, change the *-y* to *-i* and add *-er* and *-est*.

Positive	Comparative	Superlative
slow	slower	slowest
wealthy	wealthier	wealthiest
lazy	lazier	laziest
tall	taller	tallest
close	closer	closest
pretty	prettier	prettiest

Adjectives of more than one syllable usually form the comparative and superlative by adding *more* and *most*, respectively; however, there are exceptions—see *wealthy* above.

Positive	Comparative	Superlative
serious	more serious	most serious
delightful	more delightful	most delightful
worldly	more worldly	most worldly
earnest	more earnest	most earnest
plentiful	more plentiful	most plentiful
beautiful	more beautiful	most beautiful
cautious	more cautious	most cautious
intelligent	more intelligent	most intelligent
difficult	more difficult	most difficult
careful	more careful	most careful
fearful	more fearful	most fearful

There are also irregular forms of the comparative and superlative. Adjectives that describe or compare persons or things, or words that describe or compare verbs, have special forms, as illustrated below.

Positive	Comparative	Superlative
bad	worse	worst
good	better	best
much	more	most

Some adjectives cannot be compared and may be used only in the positive degree:

honest, complete, unique

EXERCISE 4.3.1

Underline the correct word in parentheses.

1. The (tall, taller, tallest) twin was the (quick, quicker, quickest) speaker.

2. Summerside is the (large, larger, largest) town in Prince Edward Island.

3. King Boy is the (fast, faster, fastest) horse in the race.

4. Helen is the (diligent, most diligent) girl in the class.

5. Rice is a (plentiful, more plentiful, most plentiful) food than carrots.

EXERCISE 4.3.2

Add the missing positive, comparative, and/or superlative degrees of comparison for the following adjectives:

	Positive	Comparative	Superlative
1.		better	
2.	careful		
3.			most delightful
4.	pretty		
5.	enjoyable		

EXERCISE 4.3.3

Underline the correct form of the adjective in parentheses. In a sentence, explain your answer.

1. Is gold or silver the (more, most) expensive?

_____

2. Irena is the (tall, taller, tallest) of the two girls.

_____

3. Summerside is one of the (more, most) beautiful eastern towns.

_____

4. My dog, Scooter, is the (fast, faster, fastest) of the three dogs.

_____

5. That sailor is the (most careful, carefullest) one on the ship.

_____

EXERCISE 4.3.4

This assignment is to be handed in to be marked. Write a paragraph of at least four sentences containing at least twelve adjectives. In a sentence after the paragraph, identify the adjectives.

_____

_____

_____

_____

_____

_____

_____

_____

_____

_____

4.4 ADVERBS

Just as adjectives describe the nouns they are modifying, adverbs usually describe the actions of verbs. An **adverb** is a word that tells how, when, where, or why something is happening. Adverbs may also describe adjectives or other adverbs. Adverbs usually (but not always) end in -_ly_ (sudden_ly_, quick_ly_, rude_ly_, ear_ly_, noisi_ly_, real_ly_).

Consider the following examples.

ADVERB MODIFYING A VERB

He swims _skilfully_.

In the above sentence, look at the verb _swims_ and ask, "_How_ does he swim?" The answer is _skilfully_. Hence, the adverb _skilfully_ in this sentence is said to modify the verb _swims_.

ADVERB MODIFYING AN ADJECTIVE

She is an _extremely_ intelligent girl.

In this sentence, turn to the adjective _intelligent_ and ask "_How_ intelligent?" The answer is, _extremely intelligent_. _Extremely_ is thus used to modify the adjective _intelligent_.

ADVERB MODIFYING AN ADVERB

He sang *very* beautifully.

In this sentence, ask *how* well he sang. *Beautifully* is an adverb modifying the verb *sang*. Then, ask *how* beautifully? The answer is *very beautifully*. Hence, *very* is an adverb that modifies the adverb *beautifully*.

While adjectives answer a question about a noun, adverbs answer question about a verb. Adverbs answer the questions How? When? or Where? about a verb. When an adverb describes an adjective or another adverb, it will also answer the same questions in reference to the word it is modifying.

■ **Examples:**

a) The choir sang beautifully.

(How did the choir sing?—beautifully)

b) The discoverers travelled inland.

(Where did the discoverers travel?—inland)

c) The NATO commanders met yesterday.

(When did they meet?—yesterday)

d) The band played extremely loudly.

(How loudly did it play?—extremely)

EXERCISE 4.4.1

Underline the adverbs in the sentences below, and in a sentence tell what word each modifies:

1. The rescuers made very little progress.

_____

2. The divers dove very quickly from the boat.

_____

3. He is quite tired.

_____

4. The injured animal walked painfully home.

_____

5. His suit fitted him perfectly.

_____

4.5 COMPARATIVE ADVERBS

Like adjectives, adverbs have three degrees of comparison: **positive**, **comparative**, and **superlative**. Use the comparative degree when you compare two things, the superlative degree when you compare three or more things.

■ **Examples:**

Positive degree:	The boy runs fast.
Comparative degree:	The dog runs faster than the boy.
Superlative degree:	The horse runs the fastest of all three.

Here is a chart showing the degrees of some regular and some less regular adverbs.

Positive	Comparative	Superlative
fast	faster	fastest
soon	sooner	soonest
badly	worse	worst
much	more	most

Note the following two similar adverbs:

far	farther	farthest	(distance that can be measured)
far	further	furthest	(mental distance that cannot be measured)

■ **Examples:**

Mardelle went farther in the race than Dennis did.

Lubna advanced further in her studies than Mary did.

Adverbs that end in *-ly* are usually compared as follows:

Positive	Comparative	Superlative
swiftly	more swiftly	most swiftly
quickly	more quickly	most quickly

EXERCISE 4.5.1

Give the degree of comparison for each of the following adverbs:

Positive	Comparative	Superlative
1. gaily		
2. well		
3. soon		
4. correctly		
5. curiously		

NOTE: As with adjectives, some adverbs cannot be compared; for example, *completely, uniquely.*

COMMON ERROR: *GOOD* AND *WELL*

Good is always used as an adjective:

> Black Beauty is a *good* horse.

> Shoshana is *good*.

> Al looks *good* in brown.

Well can be used as an adjective or an adverb. It is an adjective when it modifies a noun, and an adverb when it modifies a verb.

> Harry looks *well* today. (adjective—modifies *Harry*)

> The student read the poem *well*. (adverb—modifies *read*)

EXERCISE 4.5.2

Underline the correct word in parentheses and, in a sentence, justify your choice:

1. My dog did (good, well) at the fair.

2. People who feel (good, well) usually take (good, well) care of their health.

3. The meal smells (good, well).

4. The blue suit looks (good, well) on you.

5. I was sick yesterday, but today I feel (good, well).

EXERCISE 4.5.3

Underline the adverbs; then, in a sentence, identify what each modifies:

1. He flew westward toward the setting sun.

_____

2. I know the solution to your exceedingly troublesome problem.

_____

3. The brook runs quite smoothly now.

_____

4. The police officer spoke quietly and softly to the child, who was crying loudly and angrily.

_____

5. Soon the rain completely soaked our clothes.

_____

EXERCISE 4.5.4

Write sentences using the positive, comparative, and superlative degrees of comparison of the following adverbs:

1. quickly

_____

_____

_____

2. well

_____

_____

_____

3. soon

_____

_____

_____

4. much

_____

_____

_____

5. badly

_____

_____

_____

EXERCISE 4.5.5

Underline the correct word in parentheses and, in a sentence, justify your choice:

1. The doctors say that the child is not (good, well).

_____

2. The flowers smell (sweet, sweetly).

_____

3. He is a (real, really) famous person.

_____

4. Do you feel (strange, strangely) in this new school?

_____

5. That old man should walk (slower, slowly).

_____

ANSWER KEY

EXERCISE 4.1.1

1. *The*, *tall*, and *bearded* all modify the noun *man*; *the* and *crowded* both modify the noun *street*.
3. *The*, *tall*, and *graceful*, all modify the noun *model*; *the* modifies the noun *runway*.
5. *The*, *large*, and *dirty* all modify the noun *elephant*; *the* modifies the noun *dirt*.

EXERCISE 4.1.2

Answers will vary.

EXERCISE 4.1.3

1. *gloomy* modifies the noun subject *sky*
3. *alive* modifies the noun subject *audience*
5. *sick* modifies the noun subject *Shoshana*

EXERCISE 4.1.4

Answers will vary.

EXERCISE 4.1.5

1. French
3. Norwegian
5. Spanish

EXERCISE 4.1.6

1. *The* modifies *lions*
   two modifies *lions*
   trained modifies *lions*
   the modifies *hoop*
   large modifies *hoop*
   flaming modifies *hoop*
   their modifies *manes*

3. *Five* modifies *hours*
   a modifies *fog*
   thick modifies *fog*
   the modifies *airport*

5. *Irish* modifies *settlers*
   this modifies *country*
   huge modifies *country*
   several modifies *years*

EXERCISE 4.2.1

1. *a*, used before a word beginning with a consonant
3. *an*, used before a word beginning with a vowel
5. *a*, used before a word beginning with a consonant

EXERCISE 4.2.2

Adjective	*Modifies*
1. That	kind
the	south
far	south

3. Most   accidents
      a   caution
      little   caution
5. That   skater
      nimble   skater

EXERCISE 4.3.1

1. taller, quicker
3. fastest
5. more plentiful

EXERCISE 4.3.2

Positive	*Comparative*	*Superlative*
1. good	better	best
3. delightful	more delightful	most delightful
5. enjoyable	more enjoyable	most enjoyable

EXERCISE 4.3.3

1. more
3. most
5. most careful

Explanatory sentences will vary.

EXERCISE 4.3.4

Answers will vary.

EXERCISE 4.4.1

Adverb	*Modifies*
1. very	the adjective, little
3. quite	the adjective, tired
5. perfectly	the verb, fitted

EXERCISE 4.5.1

Positive	*Comparative*	*Superlative*
1. gaily	more gaily	most gaily
3. soon	sooner	soonest
5. curiously	more curiously	most curiously

EXERCISE 4.5.2

1. well
3. good
5. well

EXERCISE 4.5.3

Adverb	*Modifies*
1. westward	flew
3. smoothly	runs
now	runs
quite	smoothly
5. soon	soaked
completely	soaked

EXERCISE 4.5.4

	Positive	*Comparative*	*Superlative*
1.	quickly	more quickly	most quickly
3.	soon	sooner	soonest
5.	badly	more badly	most badly

Sentences will vary.

EXERCISE 4.5.5

1. well
3. really
5. slowly

Sentences will vary

1. adjective *well* modifies the noun *child*
3. adverb *really* modifies the adjective *famous*
5. adverb *slowly* modifies the verb phrase *should walk*

MODULE 5

VERBALS

Learning Outcome Statement

By successfully completing a series of module exercises, you will be able to use correctly the various verbal forms—participles, gerunds, and infinitives—consistent with the conventions of English grammar.

VERBALS

In Module 3, you were introduced to verbs. Although it is important to understand what words are verbs and how they function in sentences, it is equally important to understand what words are *not* verbs, even though at first glance, they may look like them.

Verbals are words that are derived from verbs but do not function as verbs in the sentence. There are three types of verbals:

1. participles (also known as "verbal adjectives"),

2. gerunds (also know as "verbal nouns"), and

3. infinitives.

5.1 PARTICIPLES

A **participle** is a word that looks like a verb (it indicates action), but works as an adjective. It modifies either a noun or a pronoun.

■ **Example:**

The boy, *limping* badly, is my son.

In this sentence, the word *limping* is a participle. It looks like a verb; however, in this sentence *limping* functions as an adjective, modifying or describing the noun *boy*. Which boy is the son? The boy who is limping badly.

■ **Example:**

The girl *throwing* the ball is my cousin.

Throwing functions as an adjective in this sentence. It modifies the noun *girl*.

To sum up: Participles are formed from verbs. They always modify nouns or pronouns.

EXERCISE 5.1.1

Write a sentence containing the verb form listed as a participle.

■ **Example:**

cry   The child crying is my sister.

1. sing

_____

2. blow

_____

3. play

_____

4. listen

_____

5. face

_____

TYPES OF PARTICIPLES

There are three kinds of participles: present, past, and present perfect. As stated earlier, participles are formed from verbs, but they function as adjectives; they modify nouns or pronouns.

Present Participles

Present participles end in -*ing* and refer to an action taking place at the present time.

■ **Example:**

The bees *buzzing* around the nest are angry.

The word *buzzing* is a present participle because it refers to an action that is presently happening. Notice that the participle ends in -*ing*, a suffix that indicates the present participle. *Buzzing* is a form of the verb *buzz*; however, it acts as an adjective in the sentence because it modifies the noun *bees*.

EXERCISE 5.1.2

Underline the present participle in the following sentences. In a sentence, explain the specific use of each participle.

■ **Example:**

The people *wearing* hats are police officers.

Wearing acts as an adjective because it modifies the noun *people*.

1. Children walking to school discovered the wallet.

_____

_____

2. I love to hear singing birds.

_____

_____

3. Mr. Chan watched the boy raking the leaves.

_____

_____

4. The boy sleeping in the hay is my friend.

_____

_____

5. The man wearing the mask frightened me.

_____

_____

Past Participle

A **past participle** is also a verb form that functions as an adjective. It expresses an action that is already complete. The past participle frequently ends in -*ed*, but may also end in *t* (*kept*), *n* or *ne* (*done*), or *en* (*chosen*).

A participle is always the third principal part of any verb (see section 3.4). For example: *give*, *gave*, *given*; *look*, *looked*, *looked*

◼ **Example:**

> The man *wounded* in the fall cried for help.

Wounded is a past participle. It refers to an action that has already happened and ends in -*ed*. Like the present participle, it functions as an adjective; it modifies the noun *man*.

EXERCISE 5.1.3

Write a sentence containing the past participle of the given word.

◼ **Example:**

> hid   The map *hidden* in the wall will lead us to a treasure.

1. play

_____

2. dive

_____

3. fall

_____

4. damage

_____

5. invite

_____

Present Perfect Participle

The final type of participle is a **present perfect participle**. As explained above, a past participle is a verb form that expresses an action that has already happened. When the word *having* is used with a past participle to modify a noun or a pronoun, the two words together form a present perfect participle.

■ **Example:**

> *Having found* their seats, the passengers prepared for take-off.

In this example, *having found* is a present perfect participle. (See Module 3 for a review of the present perfect tenses.) The two words work together to modify the noun *passengers* and to describe an action that has already taken place.

EXERCISE 5.1.4

Underline the present perfect participle in each of the following sentences. Then, in each case, write a sentence explaining which word it modifies.

■ **Example:**

> *Having voted* for Anton Jeyanayagam, we were sorry when he lost.

As an adjective, *having voted* modifies the pronoun *we*.

1. Never having seen the movie, Fatima was very excited.

_____

_____

2. Having finished our dinner, we did the dishes.

_____

_____

3. The salesperson, having worked all day, was glad to get home.

_____

_____

4. Having chosen a dress, Alice finished getting ready for her date.

_____

_____

5. The police officer, having caught the criminal, was congratulated by her superior.

_____

_____

COMMON ERROR—DANGLING PARTICIPLES

A **dangling participle** is a participle that does not logically modify the noun or pronoun to which it refers. As a result, the sentence will say something different from what the author had intended to say.

■ **Example:**

Having finished the dishes, the stereo was turned on.

Having finished is a present perfect participle that appears to modify *stereo*. Written correctly, the sentence would read:

■ **Example:**

Having finished the dishes, Jorge turned on the stereo.

In this example, the participle, *having finished* clearly modifies the noun Jorge. Thus, Jorge, not the stereo, finished the dishes.

EXERCISE 5.1.5

In the following sentences, identify the dangling participles, and state what they are illogically modifying. Rewrite each sentence so that the participle is not dangling.

■ **Example:**

While teaching English, a fly landed on Ms. Chan's glasses.

Here, the dangling participle *teaching* is illogically modifying the noun *fly*. (As written, the fly appears to be teaching English!)

■ **Rewritten:**

While Ms. Chan was teaching English, a fly landed on her glasses.

1. Delivering the letters, the dog bit the letter carrier.

_____

_____

_____

2. Using clever advertising, new clients can be attracted.

_____

_____

_____

3. Screaming for attention, the nanny ignored the child.

_____

_____

_____

4. Having completed the tax return on time, the client paid the accountant.

_____

_____

_____

5. Having never been in northern Canada before, Great Slave Lake was a beautiful place to go sightseeing.

_____

_____

_____

5.2   GERUNDS

A **gerund,** or **verbal noun,** is another type of verbal. Like the participle, it is formed from a verb. Like the present form of the participle, it also ends in _-ing_. Gerunds, however, act as nouns in a sentence. To refresh your memory, nouns may be used as:

    a) subjects of verbs,

    b) objects of verbs,

    c) objects of prepositions (see list of prepositions in Module 6), and

    d) complements of linking verbs (predicate noun subjective completions).

Every verb has a form that ends in _-ing_—for example, _swimming_, _running_, _taking_, and _laughing_. You have already learned that when the _-ing_ form is used as an adjective, it is called a present participle. When used as a _noun_, it is called a gerund.

■ **Example:**

    Skiing is a winter sport.

In this example, _skiing_ is a gerund. Although it can be used to express action, in this sentence it is working as a noun (_skiing_ refers to a sport, not an action). Notice that the function of _skiing_ in this sentence is as the subject of the verb _is_. As with nouns, gerunds can be subjects or objects of verbs, objects of prepositions, or predicate noun subjective completions.

■ **More examples:**

She enjoys *skating*.	*Skating* is the noun object of the verb *enjoys*.
Canada's most popular sport is *skating*.	*Skating* is the noun subjective completion of the linking verb *is*.
Saturday is the best time for *watching* baseball.	*Watching* is the noun object of the preposition *for*.

Watching also functions as a verb since it takes the direct object *baseball*.

> *NOTE:* If you have trouble remembering which word ending in *-ing* acts as an adjective and which acts as a noun, the following may help you:
>
> 1. The word *participle* contains the letter *a* (adjective).
>
> 2. The word *gerund* contains the letter *n* (noun).

EXERCISE 5.2.1

Underline the gerunds in the following sentences. In the space provided, write a sentence describing the function or relation of each: subject of the verb, object of the verb, object of the preposition, or subjective completion of the linking verb.

■ **Example:**

Baking is my favourite hobby.

The gerund is *baking*. It is the subject of the verb *is*.

1. Shovelling snow is tedious work.

_____

2. He earns extra money by delivering papers.

_____

3. I stopped playing with my friends.

_____

4. Seeing is believing.

_____

5. Laughing is good for your health.

_____

EXERCISE 5.2.2

Write a sentence containing a gerund, as directed.

■ **Example:**

Swimming as subjective completion.

> My favourite sport is swimming.

Swimming is a gerund used as a noun subjective completion of the linking verb *is*.

1. *cook* as the object of the verb

_____

2. *act* as the subject of the verb

_____

3. *jog* as the object of a preposition

_____

4. *play* as a subjective completion

_____

5. *lie* as the subject of the verb

_____

5.3 INFINITIVES

The final type of verbal is called an **infinitive**. An infinitive is made up of the word *to* and a verb form, for example: *to swim, to catch, to jump*. It is formed from a verb, but functions in a sentence as a noun, adjective *or* adverb, depending on its use. Able to function in these ways, the infinitive is more versatile than a participle, which functions only as an adjective, or a gerund, which functions only as a noun.

When acting as a noun, an infinitive can be the subject of a verb, the object of a verb, or the subjective completion. It cannot be the object of a preposition. The word *to* is a preposition, and one cannot have two prepositions in a row. (See Module 6 for further information about prepositions.)

The sentences below illustrate infinitives that function as nouns:

> 1. *To skate* well requires much practice.

(*To skate* is an infinitive functioning as the subject of the verb *requires*.)

> 2. I like *to dance* frequently.

(*To dance* is an infinitive functioning as the object of the verb *like*.)

> 3. *To teach* a subject is *to instruct* someone.

(*To teach* is an infinitive functioning as the subject of the verb *is* and *to instruct* is an infinitive functioning as subjective completion of the linking verb *is*.)

EXERCISE 5.3.1

In the sentences below, underline the infinitives. Tell how each is used: as a noun, adjective, or adverb. Give the full relationship of each.

■ **Examples:**

I had <u>to organize</u> the bridal shower.
To organize is an infinitive used as a noun, object of the verb *had*.

You would be wise <u>to do</u> your homework.
To do is an infinitive used as an adverb, modifying the adjective *wise*.

1. Most of our class like to go on trips.

_____

_____

2. The first thing that we had to do was to organize.

_____

_____

3. To refuse was considered impolite.

_____

_____

4. We planned to buy the food.

_____

_____

5. To err is human; to forgive, divine.

_____

_____

EXERCISE 5.3.2

Write sentences using the following infinitives as requested.

1. *to go* as the subject of the verb

_____

2. *to move* as a subjective completion

_____

3. *to run* as the object of the verb

_____

4. *to jump* as a subjective completion

_____

5. *to hide* as the object of the verb

_____

Infinitives can also act as *adjectives* or *adverbs*. If they modify or describe nouns, they are used as adjectives. If they modify verbs, adjectives, or adverbs, they are used as adverbs.

■ **Examples:**

    1. He wanted a place to store his furniture.

To store is an infinitive used as an adjective, modifying the noun *place*.

    2. We should stay home to study.

To study is an infinitive used as an adverb, modifying the verb *should stay*.

    3. He is wise to read philosophy and psychology.

To read is an infinitive used as an adverb, modifying the adjective *wise*.

EXERCISE 5.3.3

In the following sentences, underline the infinitives. In a sentence, state how each is being used (as an adjective, adverb, or noun), and give its relationship.

■ **Examples:**

    We had a chance <u>to win</u>.

To win is an infinitive used as an adjective modifying the noun *chance*.

1. *Moby Dick* is a book to enjoy.

_____

_____

2. He waved a handkerchief to gain her attention.

_____

_____

3. We remained after school to practise.

_____

_____

4. The best way to see the Maritime provinces is by car.

_____

_____

5. Canadians should travel to appreciate their own country.

_____

_____

EXERCISE 5.3.4

Write a sentence according to the instructions provided. In a sentence, explain your answer.

■ **Example:**

to burn as an adjective

The campers looked for dry wood to burn.

To burn is an infinitive. It is used as an adjective modifying the noun *wood*.

1. *to inquire* as an adverb

_____

_____

_____

2. *to learn* as an adverb

_____

_____

_____

3. *to see* as an adjective

_____

_____

_____

4. *to fly* as an adjective

_____

_____

_____

5. *to go* as a noun

_____

_____

_____

ANSWER KEY

EXERCISE 5.1.1

Answers will vary.

EXERCISE 5.1.2

Sentences will vary.
1. *walking*—modifies *children*
3. *raking*—modifies *boy*
5. *wearing*—modifies *man*

EXERCISE 5.1.3

Answers will vary. The past participles of the given verbs are as follows:
1. played
3. fallen
5. invited

EXERCISE 5.1.4

1. *having seen*
   adjective—modifies the subject noun *Fatima*
3. *having worked*
   adjective—modifies the subject noun *salesperson*
5. *having caught*
   adjective—modifies the subject noun *police officer*

EXERCISE 5.1.5

Rewritten sentences will vary.
1. *delivering*—*dog*
3. *screaming*—*nanny*
5. *having been*—*Great Slave Lake*

EXERCISE 5.2.1

1. *shovelling*, subject of the verb *is*
3. *playing*, object of the verb *stopped*
5. *laughing*, subject of the verb *is*

EXERCISE 5.2.2

Answers will vary.

EXERCISE 5.3.1

1. *to go*, noun, object of the verb *like*
3. *to refuse*, noun, subject of the verb phrase *was considered*
5. *to err*, noun, subject of the verb *is*
   to forgive, noun, subject of the verb *is* (understood)

EXERCISE 5.3.2

Answers will vary.

EXERCISE 5.3.3

1. *to enjoy*, adjective, modifying the noun *book*
3. *to practise*, adverb, modifying the verb *remained*
5. *to appreciate*, adverb, modifying the verb phrase *should travel*

EXERCISE 5.3.4

Answers will vary.

MODULE 6

PREPOSITIONS AND CONJUNCTIONS

Learning Outcome Statement

By successfully completing a series of module exercises, you will be able to use prepositions and the various types of conjunctions in ways that are consistent with the conventions of English grammar.

PREPOSITIONS AND CONJUNCTIONS

6.1 PREPOSITIONS

In Module 1, you were introduced to prepositions while learning the case and relation of nouns. Now it is time for you to learn the use, or function, of prepositions.

A **preposition** is a word that introduces a group of words, known as a prepositional phrase. (See Module 7, "Phrases.") That group of words must not contain within it a subject or a verb. It must, however, contain a noun (or pronoun) that completes the preposition and is said to be its object.

A preposition is used to link and show the relationship between its object and some other word in a given sentence. For example, in the sentence, "The dog crawled *under* the fence," the preposition *under* links its object *fence* to the verb *crawled*. It tells where the dog crawled. All prepositions join their objects to another word in a given sentence.

COMMON PREPOSITIONS

Although there are approximately 100 prepositions in the English language, those most commonly used are listed below:

about	before	during	off	to
above	behind	except	on	toward
across	below	for	onto	under
after	beneath	from	out	until
against	beside	in	outside	up
along	between	inside	over	upon
among	beyond	into	past	with
around	by	near	since	without
at	down	of	through	

NOTE: Although the preposition *during* ends in *-ing*, it is neither a verb nor a verbal.

EXERCISE 6.1.1

In sentence form, identify the prepositions and their objects in the spaces provided. (There is more than one preposition in most of the sentences.)

■ **Example:**

The ship in the river rushed to the shore.

The first preposition is *in*; its object, *river*. The second preposition is *to*; its object, *shore*. In this sentence, the first preposition *in* shows the relationship between its object *river* and the subject *ship*. The second preposition *to*, shows the relationship between its object *shore* and the verb *rushed*.

1. The miners in the mine worked in shifts.

_____

_____

2. The Canadian Parliament meets in the city of Ottawa.

_____

_____

3. He delivered the paper to the red house on the corner.

_____

_____

4. The arrow landed in the centre of the target.

_____

_____

5. The ducks waddled along the side of the road.

_____

_____

EXERCISE 6.1.2

In the following sentences underline the prepositions once and their objects twice. Then circle the word to which each preposition relates.

■ **Example:**

He went to the teacher to get some paper for his test.

1. The squirrel in our yard is friendly with the whole family.

2. Close the door tightly when you come for a visit at noon.

3. Are you going to the store for groceries?

4. Do you not care about the writing of the examination?

5. What a wonderful day in the woods it has been!

PREPOSITION OR ADVERB?

You may sometimes wonder when the same word is an adverb and when it is a preposition. Consider the following examples:

He stood *outside.* (adverb)

He stood *outside* the building. (preposition)

He walked *around.* (adverb)

He walked *around* the building. (preposition)

The general rule is that if you add a noun or pronoun object to an adverb, you convert it into a preposition. If you remove a noun object from a preposition, you convert the preposition into an adverb. Similarly, *outside* and *around* may be either adverbs or prepositions, depending on their use.

6.2   CONJUNCTIONS

Conjunctions are words that join words, phrases (see Module 7), or clauses (see Module 8). There are three main types of conjunctions: coordinate, correlative, and subordinate.

COORDINATE CONJUNCTIONS

A **coordinate conjunction** is a word that joins or separates words, phrases, or clauses *of the same grammatical value.* For instance, a coordinate conjunction may join nouns with nouns, verbs with verbs, adverbs with adverbs, adjectives with adjectives, phrases with phrases, or clauses with clauses. The most common coordinate conjunctions are *and*, *but*, *or*, *nor*, and *for*.

■ **Examples:**

1. Boys *and* girls exercise in the playground.

And is a coordinate conjunction. It connects the two nouns, *boys* and *girls*, thereby forming a *compound subject*. (See Module 9, "Sentences.")

2. The children shouted *and* sang in the street.

Here, *and* is a coordinate conjunction, connecting the two verbs *shouted* and *sang*. This connection creates a *compound verb* or *predicate*.

3. Cattle graze in the valley *but* not on the hilltop.

But is used here as a coordinate conjunction. It connects the two phrases of equal grammatical value, *in the valley* and *on the hilltop*. (For further information on phrases, see Module 7.)

4. You must study *or* you will not succeed.

In this example *or* is a coordinate conjunction connecting two principal or independent clauses (see Module 8), *you must study* and *you will not succeed*.

5. She said that she would attend the meeting *and* that she would be on time.

This time *and* is a *coordinate conjunction* connecting the two subordinate or dependent clauses (see Module 8) *that she would attend the meeting* and *that she would be on time*.

CORRELATIVE CONJUNCTIONS

Correlative conjunctions are coordinate conjunctions that work together in pairs to join or separate words or word groups of the same grammatical value. The most common correlatives are *both/and*, *either/or*, *neither/nor*, and *not only/but also*. Note that each half of a correlative conjunction must be followed by the same part of speech.

■ **Examples:**

> 1. *Either* Regina *or* Saskatoon is the capital of Saskatchewan.

Either/or are correlative conjunctions connecting the two nouns *Regina* and *Saskatoon*.

> 2. You will find him *neither* on the roof *nor* in the gym.

Neither/nor are correlative conjunctions connecting the two prepositional word groups *on the roof* and *in the gym*.

> 3. *Not only* salt *but also* pepper is on the table.

Not only/but also are correlative conjunctions connecting the two nouns *salt* and *pepper*.

> *NOTE:* Be careful with the number agreement between subject and verb when using correlative conjunctions. The verb *must* agree in number with its nearer subject.

■ **Examples:**

> 1. Neither his father nor his <u>sisters</u> *are* coming.

Since the nearer subject is *sisters* (plural), the verb must also be plural (*are coming*, not *is coming*).

> 2. Neither his sisters nor his <u>father</u> *is* coming.

Since the nearer subject is *father* (singular), the verb must also be singular (*is coming*, not *are coming*).

SUBORDINATE CONJUNCTIONS

Unlike coordinate conjunctions, which join words, phrases, or clauses of like grammatical value, **subordinate conjunctions** introduce subordinate (dependent) clauses. A subordinate clause is connected by its subordinate conjunction to another word or clause. (See Module 8, "Clauses.") Principal clauses make sense by themselves and can stand on their own. Subordinate clauses do not make sense by themselves and cannot stand alone (see Module 8).

■ **Example:**

> He passed the test with ease *because* he was well prepared.

Because is a subordinate conjunction. It connects the subordinate clause *because he was well prepared* to the main clause *he passed the test with ease*.

In Module 8, the function of the subordinate conjunction will become clearer. At this point, you should simply become familiar with the more common subordinate conjunctions in the following list.

after	because	so that	until
although	before	that	when
as	in order that	though	whenever
as if	since	unless	where
whether	which	while	who (whom)

Subordinate conjunctions have several functions that will be made clearer in Module 8. At this point, though, it is necessary for you to know a little about one special kind of subordinate conjunction: the **relative pronoun**.

Relative Pronouns as Conjunctions

Observe the following sentences:

1. The woman *who* just came in is my aunt.

2. He signed the report, *which* I gave him yesterday.

3. The dog *that* is howling in the yard is unhappy.

In the first example, the relative pronoun *who* is related to the noun *woman*. It joins the group of words *who just came in* to the noun subject *woman*.

In the second example the relative pronoun *which* is related to the noun *report*. It joins the group of words *which I gave him yesterday* to the noun object *report*.

In the third example, the relative pronoun *that* is related to the noun *dog*. It joins the group of words *that is howling in the yard* to the noun subject *dog*.

The Difference Between a Subordinate Conjunction and a Preposition

Subordinate conjunctions and prepositions both introduce groups of words. Prepositional word groups must not contain subjects or verbs, but must contain objects. Subordinate conjunction word groups, on the other hand, must contain subjects and verbs but do not necessarily require objects.

■ Examples:

1. I saw him in school.

Here, the preposition *in* takes the obligatory object, in this case the word *school*. The phrase itself, however, has no subject or verb within it.

2. As I was walking down the street, I witnessed a murder.

In this example, the subordinate conjunction *as* is followed by the subject pronoun *I* and the verb phrase *was walking*. Moreover, the verb *was walking* has no object.

To sum up, prepositional phrases have objects but no subjects or verbs; clauses must have subjects and verbs, but may or may not have objects.

EXERCISE 6.2.1

Using the different types of conjunctions you have studied, write sentences that combine the following pair (or groups) of sentences into a single sentence. In a sentence, explain the type of conjunction you used.

NOTE: Be sure you have a mixture of coordinate, correlative, and subordinate conjunctions.

■ **Examples:**

> We ran to catch the bus. It had already left.
>
> We ran to catch the bus, but it had already left.

NOTE: But is a coordinate conjunction.

1. It was early morning. The dew had not yet disappeared.

_____

2. The spring weather was unfavourable. The summer brought rain. The crops revived.

_____

3. The police took up the search for the little boy. The neighbours did also.

_____

4. He served his country nobly. He went down with his ship.

_____

5. Lee wanted to go to the concert. Stuart was too tired to go with her.

_____

EXERCISE 6.2.2

In the sentences below, underline all conjunctions. Then, in sentence form, state the type of each, and the word or words to which each is connected.

1. Although I seldom eat peas, I sometimes make exceptions.

2. The woman who lives next door is my mother's aunt.

3. Not only parcels but also letters were jammed into the mailbox.

4. Because a heavy snow has fallen overnight, I shall not go to the office this morning.

5. I am ill, but my brother will represent me in the meeting.

EXERCISE 6.2.3

Use the following words in sentences, first as a preposition and second as a conjunction. Then, in sentence form, state the difference between a preposition and a conjunction.

1. after

2. before

3. since

_____

_____

Difference between a preposition and a conjunction:

_____

_____

WRITING ASSIGNMENT

May be handed in to your instructor.

Using the facts below, write a one-paragraph story. In your story, include the material that you have learned in Modules 5 and 6: participles, gerunds, infinitives, prepositions, and conjunctions. Underline these in your story and be prepared to discuss them with your instructor.

Facts for composing your story:

My brother and I ramble through the woods.

We discover a deserted house.

We enter.

We become separated.

I look out the window and see my brother running away.

What I did.

_____

_____

_____

_____

_____

_____

_____

_____

_____

_____

ANSWER KEY

EXERCISE 6.1.1

1. The first preposition is *in*; its object is *mine*.
   The second preposition is *in*; its object is *shifts*.
3. preposition *to*; object *house*
   preposition *on*; object *corner*
5. preposition *along*; object *side*
   preposition *of*; object *road*

EXERCISE 6.1.2

1. The (squirrel) in our <u>yard</u> is (friendly) with the whole <u>family</u>.

3. Are you (going) to the <u>store</u> <u>for</u> <u>groceries</u>?

5. What a wonderful (day) in the <u>woods</u> it has been!

EXERCISE 6.2.1

Although answers will vary, here are a few suggestions:
1. As it was early morning, the dew had not yet disappeared.
3. Not only the police but also the neighbours took up the search for the little boy.
5. Lee wanted to go to the concert, but Stuart was too tired to go with her.

EXERCISE 6.2.2

1. *Although* is a subordinate conjunction connected to the verb *make*.
3. *Not only ... but also* are correlative conjunctions joining the two nouns *parcels* and *letters*.
5. *But* is a coordinate conjunction joining the two word groups *I am ill* and *my brother will represent me in the meeting*.

EXERCISE 6.2.3

Answers will vary but note the following:
After, *before*, and *since*, when used as prepositions, must be followed by noun objects. Their word groups must not contain either a subject or a verb. When used as conjunctions, these three words must be followed by subjects and verbs.

Examples:
After the rain, we went outside to play. (preposition)
After I had waited for hours, I gave up and went home. (conjunction)
Before dark, we went home. (preposition)
Before the light faded, we went home (conjunction)
Since the day that war ended, I have been happy. (preposition)
Since it is raining, let us stay inside the house. (conjunction)

Difference:
A preposition must be followed by an object and must not contain within its word group a subject or verb. A conjunction may or may not be followed by an object, but must contain within its word group both a subject and a verb.

Writing Assignment Number 1

This is a hand-in exercise.

MODULE

7

PHRASES

Learning Outcome Statement

By successfully completing a series of module exercises, you will be able to:

a) identify prepositional, participial (present and past), gerund, and infinitive phrases;

b) understand clearly the roles that such phrases play in sentences;

c) know the relationship of each phrase to other parts of speech in sentences; and

d) enrich and colour your own writing as you practise the correct uses of phrases.

PHRASES

A **phrase** is a group of words that has the grammatical value of a single word, and that contains neither a subject nor a verb. You have already learned that a verb phrase is a verb containing more than one word, for example, *shall have been working*, *will have worked*, and *should be doing*. More specifically, in this module, *a phrase is a group of words containing neither subjects nor predicates* (see Modules 1 and 3). No phrase can stand alone, since it does not express a complete thought.

To help you understand and correctly use phrases, this module will:

1. define each type of phrase,

2. illustrate the composition of each phrase to be studied through examples and practical exercises,

3. describe the analysis of sentences containing each type of phrase, and

4. familiarize you with the creative use of all phrases studied by having you write sentences and short compositions.

One purpose of phrases is to add colour and imaginative content. They are also used to make clearer and more specific the words they modify, thereby creating better understanding for the reader.

In this module we shall examine in detail the following four types of phrases: prepositional phrases, participial phrases, gerund phrases, and infinitive phrases.

7.1   PREPOSITIONAL PHRASES

Prepositional phrases usually function as adjectives (to modify nouns or pronouns) or as adverbs (to modify verbs, adjectives, or other adverbs).

■ **Example:**

> Gitti went to the store.

In this sentence, *to the store* is a single unit that describes where Gitti went. This phrase begins with the preposition *to*. As the word *store* answers the question *to what?*, it is the object of the preposition. As you will recall from Module 4, the definite article *the* is also an adjective, modifying the noun *store*.

Some common prepositions used as introductory words beginning a prepositional phrase are listed below. The words in **bold** can also be used as subordinate conjunctions.

above	**before**	for*	on	toward
across	behind	from	onto	under
after	below	in	over	up
among	beside	in spite of	past	upon
around	between	into	**since**	**until**
as	by	like	through	with

| at | during | near | till | without |
| because of | except | of | to ** | |

> **NOTES:** * *For* can also be used as a coordinate conjunction.
> ** *To* can also be used as part of an infinitive.

EXERCISE 7.1.1

Underline each prepositional phrase. Circle each preposition. Draw an arrow to show the word to which the phrase refers. The total number of phrases is given in square brackets [ ] at the end of each sentence.

■ **Examples:**

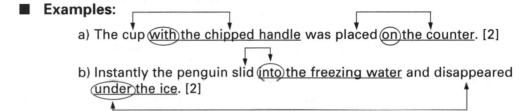

a) The cup (with) the chipped handle was placed (on) the counter. [2]

b) Instantly the penguin slid (into) the freezing water and disappeared (under) the ice. [2]

1. Through the streets and up the hill they ran. [2]

2. The guest with the red and green striped coat was pushed into the bushes behind him by his angry host. [4]

3. The red-winged blackbird builds its nest on the ground among the rushes beside a stream. [3]

4. A tall, thin stranger with curly black hair bumped into me at the grocery store. [3]

5. During the night, the milk in the bottle turned into ice. [3]

EXERCISE 7.1.2

Underline each prepositional phrase and circle the preposition. Then draw an arrow to the word each phrase modifies. Indicate whether each phrase is used as an adjective or an adverb.

■ **Examples:**

a) The green jacket (on) the hall stand is mine.   (adjective)

b) (After) the movie, let us drive (by) the river.   (adverb) (adverb)

c) Masoud and Jose raced (to) the top (of) the hill. (adverb) (adjective)

1. The antique tapestry is hanging on the wall in the lobby.

2. We are planning a visit to the zoo.

3. Many of our neighbours have summer cottages in Muskoka.

4. Did you stay in that cabin near the waterfall?

5. After dinner the whole family strolled in the park.

EXERCISE 7.1.3

a) Use each of the following prepositional phrases in a sentence.

b) Identify how you have used each phrase by writing "adjective" or "adverb" after each sentence.

c) State, in sentence form, which word(s) the phrase modifies.

■ **Example:**

except Fred

Everyone <u>except Fred</u> was enjoying the party. [adjective]

The prepositional phrase *except Fred* modifies the pronoun *everyone*.

1. in every way

_____

_____

2. about the report

_____

_____

3. through good times and bad

_____

_____

4. on the rocks

_____

_____

5. among friends

_____

_____

EXERCISE 7.1.4

This exercise should be handed in to your instructor for correction.

In approximately 75 words describe "The Most Beautiful Scene I Can Recall." Include *at least six examples* of prepositional phrases, three used as adjectives and three used as adverbs. Underline each prepositional phrase used and indicate in the margin whether the phrase has been used as an adjective or adverb.

_____

_____

_____

_____

_____

_____

_____

_____

_____

_____

_____

_____

_____

_____

_____

_____

_____

7.2 PARTICIPIAL PHRASES

In Module 5 we discussed verbal forms. One of these forms was the participle. We shall now extend that concept to participial phrases. A **participial phrase** consists of either a present participle (a verbal ending in *-ing*) or a past participle (a verbal ending in *-ed* for regular verbs and *-en*, *-ne*, or *-pt*, for irregular verbs) plus all of its modifiers (see Module 3).

Think of participial phrases as single units of grammar. They are used as adjectives and modify nouns or pronouns.

COMMON ERROR—MISPLACED/DANGLING PARTICIPIAL PHRASES

To avoid making common writing errors, such as dangling participles or misplaced modifiers (see Module 5), always place the participial phrase as close as possible to the word it logically modifies.

EXERCISE 7.2.1

Underline the present and past participial phrases in the following sentences. Draw an arrow to the word that each phrase modifies.

■ **Examples:**

a) <u>Driving in Formula Two races</u>, he not only gets his thrills but often earns a lot of prize money.

b) <u>Satisfied with his test results</u>, the student went home with a smile on his face.

1. Looking pale, the heroine gazed at the dead body in the library.

2. Having stolen all the gold watches and rings from the showcase, the thief slammed the door.

3. Missing the bus by a second, we decided to take a taxi.

4. The student waiting in your office has a few questions to ask.

5. Loaded down with groceries, my son staggered into the front hall.

EXERCISE 7.2.2

In the following sentences, put parentheses ( ) around each participial phrase. Then draw an arrow from the phrase to the word it modifies.

■ **Example:**

(Running into the house), Mary tripped on the torn carpet in the vestibule.

1. For an entire afternoon, I sat waiting for the phone to ring.

2. A tool used in cutting fine materials broke yesterday.

3. Digging in my garden, I discovered a silver ring.

4. The lion on the rock sat licking its paws.

5. Bewildered by their lack of enthusiasm, the speaker began to shuffle her notes.

EXERCISE 7.2.3

Use each of the following participial phrases in a sentence.

1. not understanding the task before her

_____

_____

2. frightened by the doctor's diagnosis

_____

_____

3. watching the children at play

_____

_____

4. overcome with sorrow

_____

_____

5. struggling to control his temper

_____

_____

EXERCISE 7.2.4

Incorporating at least five examples of participial phrases, write approximately 75 words, in the space provided below, about your favourite leisure time activity. Underline all participial phrases. Draw arrows from the phrases to the words they modify.

_____

_____

_____

_____

_____

_____

_____

_____

_____

_____

_____

_____

_____

_____

_____

_____

_____

_____

7.3 GERUND PHRASES

A **gerund phrase** is made up of a gerund (or verbal noun) plus its modifiers/complements. (See Module 5 for a discussion of gerunds.) Gerund phrases are used only as nouns. As nouns, they may function as:

1. subjects of verbs,

2. objects of verbs or objects of infinitives,

3. objects of prepositions, or

4. predicate noun subjective completions (complements) of linking verbs.

> **NOTE:** Remember that a gerund, like a participle, is a verbal ending in *-ing*. To avoid confusion, you must determine the function of the *-ing* word in order to know whether it is a participle or a gerund (see Module 5). You have already learned in this module that participial phrases act only as adjectives. Gerund phrases act only as nouns. To help you remember which *-ing* word is a participle (with adjectival value) and which is a gerund (with noun value):
>
> 1. Think of the *a* in the word "participle" as standing for "adjective."
>
> 2. Think of the *n* in the word geru*n*d as standing for "noun."

EXERCISE 7.3.1

In the following sentences, underline every gerund phrase and, in a sentence, state how each phrase is related to the rest of the sentence.

■ **Examples:**

a) <u>Reading all of the confusing assembly instructions</u> produced feelings of frustration and annoyance.

The gerund phrase *Reading all of the confusing assembly instructions* is the subject of the verb *produced*.

b) My cousin, Antonio, tried <u>playing the viola</u> in the school orchestra.

The gerund phrase *playing the viola* is the object of the verb *tried*.

c) By <u>writing constantly</u> Lena is noticing a big improvement in her English grades.

The gerund phrase *writing constantly* is the object of the preposition, *by*.

d) Our main reason for <u>taking this computer course</u> is <u>seeking to acquire new marketable skills</u>.

The phrase *taking this computer course* is the object of the preposition *for*. The phrase *seeking to acquire new marketable skills* is the noun subjective completion (complement) of the linking verb *is*.

e) Hsiu-Ju seems to enjoy <u>running on the beach</u>.

The gerund phrase *running on the beach* is the object of the infinitive *to enjoy*.

1. Walking for twenty minutes daily is excellent exercise.

_____

_____

_____

2. The children enjoyed speaking French with their nanny.

_____

_____

_____

3. Rich's favourite pastime is hiking in the mountains.

_____

_____

_____

4. The writer Thoreau placed great value on living simply.

_____

_____

_____

5. Thrilled with her excellent college exam results, my daughter began applying to several graduate schools.

_____

_____

_____

EXERCISE 7.3.2

Write sentences using the following gerund phrases as indicated. In full sentences, explain their grammatical use.

1. exercising at the health club (subject of the verb)

_____

_____

2. leaving at night (object of the preposition)

_____

_____

3. visiting the dentist twice a year (object of the verb)

_____

_____

4. learning all four classes of phrases (subject of the verb)

_____

_____

5. jumping on the trampoline (object of the verb)

_____

_____

EXERCISE 7.3.3

1. Demonstrate your knowledge of gerund phrases by writing approximately 100 words on the subject "An Event that Changed My Life." Be sure that you include at least one example each of a gerund phrase used as:

   a) subject of a verb,
   b) object of a verb,
   c) object of a preposition, and
   d) subjective completion (complement) after a linking verb.

2. Underline your gerund phrases.

3. Above each phrase, state its function.

_____

_____

_____

_____

_____

_____

_____

_____

_____

_____

_____

_____

_____

_____

_____

_____

_____

_____

7.4   INFINITIVE PHRASES

An infinitive is recognized by its form. It starts with the word *to* followed by a verb form (see Module 5).

■ **Examples:**

to talk (present)

to have talked (present perfect)

to be seen (present)

to have been seen (present perfect)

Infinitive phrases, like both prepositional and participial phrases already examined, can be used as adjectives to modify nouns or pronouns. They can also be used as adverbs to modify verbs, adjectives, or other adverbs. Moreover, they can also be used as nouns, functioning as subjects of verbs, objects of verbs, or subjective completions (complements) following linking verbs.

EXERCISE 7.4.1

In the following sentences,

a) underline the infinitive phrases,

b) state how each infinitive phrase is being used (as a noun, adjective, or adverb),

c) give the relationship of each phrase in its sentence.

■ **Examples:**

   a) James trained <u>to be a prize fighter</u>.

To be a prize fighter is an infinitive phrase used as an adverb, modifying the verb *trained*.

   b) <u>To excel in the field of biological research</u> is Yoko's main career goal.

The underlined infinitive phrase is used as a noun, subject of the verb *is*.

1. Behind the wooden fence is the best place to plant flowering shrubs.

   _____

   _____

2. She danced to win the prize.

   _____

   _____

3. Tim brought a notebook to lend me.

   _____

   _____

4. To swim well demands much practice.

   _____

   _____

5. Enrico's puppy loves to visit the vet.

   _____

   _____

EXERCISE 7.4.2

Use a table to describe the use and relationship of each infinitive phrase in the following sentences.

■ **Examples:**

   a) To run daily is healthy.

   b) No one had time to complete the bonus problem.

   c) Babies normally attempt to walk at the age of six months.

Infinitive Phrase	Use	Relationship
a) to run daily	noun	subject of the verb *is*
b) to complete the bonus problem	adjective	modifies the noun *time*
c) to walk at the age of six months	noun	object of the verb *attempt*

1. Gina's reasons were hard to understand at first.

Infinitive Phrase	Use	Relationship

2. They tried to speak French.

Infinitive Phrase	Use	Relationship

3. We ran to catch the train.

Infinitive Phrase	Use	Relationship

4. A waiter's job is to serve a table.

Infinitive Phrase	Use	Relationship

5. To play for the Montreal Canadiens was my daughter's great ambition.

Infinitive Phrase	Use	Relationship

EXERCISE 7.4.3

Write an interesting sentence using each infinitive phrase as the part of speech indicated. Draw an arrow from the infinitive phrase to the word that it modifies.

1. to love him (noun)

_____

2. to cooperate fully (adverb)

_____

3. to dance with (adjective)

_____

4. to acquire wealth and fame (adverb)

_____

5. to become a world-class soprano (noun)

_____

EXERCISE 7.4.4

a) Demonstrate your understanding of the infinitive phrase by writing approximately 75 words on the subject "The Happiest Day of My Life."

b) Include at least three infinitive phrases, illustrating all three functions of such phrases: noun, adjective, and adverb.

c) Underline each infinitive phrase used. Above each, specify its part of speech value.

_____

_____

_____

_____

_____

_____

_____

_____

_____

_____

_____

_____

_____

_____

_____

_____

ANSWER KEY

EXERCISE 7.1.1

1. Through the streets and up the hill they ran. [2]

3. The redwing blackbird builds its nest on the ground among the rushes beside a stream. [3]

5. During the night, the milk in the bottle turned into ice. [3]

EXERCISE 7.1.2

1. The antique tapestry is hanging on the wall in the lobby. [adverb] [adjective]

3. Many of our neighbours have summer cottages in Muskoka. [adjective] [adverb]

5. After dinner, the whole family strolled in the park. [adverb] [adverb]

EXERCISE 7.1.3

Answers will vary.

EXERCISE 7.1.4

Hand in for correction.

EXERCISE 7.2.1

1. Looking pale, the frightened heroine gazed at the dead body in the library.

3. Missing the bus by a second, we decided to take a taxi.

5. Loaded down with groceries, my son staggered into the front hall.

EXERCISE 7.2.2

1. For an entire afternoon, I sat (waiting for the phone to ring).

3. (Digging in my garden), I discovered a silver ring.

5. (Bewildered by their lack of enthusiasm), the speaker began to shuffle her notes.

EXERCISE 7.2.3

Answers will vary.

EXERCISE 7.2.4

Answers will vary

EXERCISE 7.3.1

1. Walking for twenty minutes daily is excellent exercise.
   The gerund phrase is subject of the verb *is*.
3. Rich's favourite pastime is hiking in the mountains.
   The phrase is the subjective completion (complement) of the verb *is*.

5. Thrilled with her excellent college exam results, my daughter began <u>applying to several graduate schools</u>.
The phrase is object of the verb *began*.

EXERCISE 7.3.2

Answers will vary.

EXERCISE 7.3.3

Answers will vary. Hand in to your instructor for marking.

EXERCISE 7.4.1

Phrase	Use	Relationship
1. to plant flowering shrubs	adjective	modifies the noun *place*
3. to lend to me	adjective	modifies the noun *notebook*
5. to visit the vet	noun	object of the verb *loves*

EXERCISE 7.4.2

Phrase	Use	Relationship
1. to understand at first	adverb	modifies the adjective *hard*
3. to catch the train	adverb	modifies the verb *ran*
5. To play for the Montreal Canadiens	noun	subject of the verb *was*

EXERCISE 7.4.3

Answers will vary.

EXERCISE 7.4.4

Answers will vary.

MODULE

CLAUSES

Learning Outcome Statement

By successfully completing a series of module exercises, you will be able to identify and use the different kinds of clauses.

CLAUSES

A sentence that contains one subject and one predicate is called a simple sentence. (See Module 9, "Sentences.") A **clause** is simply a part of a sentence that contains a subject and a predicate. This module will deal with the two types of clauses:

1. main (also known as "principle" or "independent")

2. subordinate (also known as "dependent")

It will also look at the different kinds of subordinate clauses. Finally, the module will address the function or relationship of these clauses in sentences.

In order to write more elaborate sentences, you need to understand the importance of the clause. A more elaborate sentence structure is necessary to add greater detail and a smoother flow to your writing. It is also necessary to cut down on unnecessary words, and to add variety of length to your sentences. This should improve your writing style, and thus increase the interest of your readers.

8.1   TYPES OF CLAUSES

A clause is a group of closely related words that has both a bare subject (plus modifiers) and a bare predicate or verb (plus modifiers). In other words, a clause must have a subject and a verb.

Generally speaking, if a clause makes sense on its own, it is a main clause. (See below for exceptions with some noun clauses.) If a clause does not make sense on its own, then it is a subordinate clause and will rely on the main clause for its complete meaning. We shall discuss both main and subordinate clauses in greater detail.

MAIN (PRINCIPAL) CLAUSES

A **main**, or **principal**, **clause** is independent of all other clauses (with one exception to be discussed later). The majority of main clauses can stand alone because they almost always express a complete thought.

■ **Example:**

It did not snow until after we reached home.

It did not snow is the main clause because it expresses the main idea in the sentence and can stand alone as a unit. Notice that it contains a subject (*it*) and a verb (*did not*).

SUBORDINATE CLAUSES

A **subordinate clause** is less important to the meaning of a sentence than is its principal clause. It requires the help of the principal clause to make its meaning clear. It cannot stand alone as a sentence. Subordinate conjunctions (see Module 6) or relative pronouns (see Module 2) are used to introduce subordinate clauses and must be followed by a subject and a verb. They are also used to show the relationship between the subordinate clause and the principal clause. Since subordinate clauses begin with either conjunctions or relative pronouns, they are fairly easy to recognize and identify.

■ **Example:**

It did not snow <u>until after we reached home</u>.

Until after we reached home is a subordinate clause because:

    a) It is less important to the meaning of the sentence than is the principal clause.

    b) As it is not a complete thought; it cannot stand alone, but is dependent on the principal clause *It did not snow* to complete its meaning.

    c) The clause is introduced by the subordinate conjunction *until*, followed by the subject *we* and the verb *reached*.

In the following sentences, the principal clause is underlined once and the subordinate clause is underlined twice.

    1. <u>Carol knew Galina</u>, <u>who won the race</u>.
         principal clause   subordinate clause

Carol knew Galina, a complete thought in itself, is the main or independent clause. *Who won the race* depends on the principal clause for its meaning. Note also that both clauses have subjects and verbs: *Carol* and *knew*, and *who* and *won*. Moreover, *who* is a relative pronoun, used as both the pronoun subject and the conjunction that introduces the subordinate clause.

    2. <u>After the game had ended</u>, <u>we went out for dinner</u>.
         subordinate clause   principal clause

We went out for dinner expresses a complete thought and can stand alone as a principal clause. *After the game had ended* depends on the principal clause to make sense. Again, both clauses have subjects and verbs: *game* and *had ended*, and *we* and *went*. Moreover, *After* is a conjunction that introduces the subordinate clause.

    3. <u>We waited inside</u> <u>until the rain had stopped</u>.
         principal clause   subordinate clause

By using the explanations in examples 1 and 2 above, you should now be able to explain why *We waited inside* is the main clause and why *until the rain had stopped* is the subordinate clause introduced by the conjunction *until*.

    4. <u>He went to the store</u> <u>because he needed bread</u>.
         principal clause   subordinate clause

Why have the clauses been identified in this way?

    5. <u>When I saw the girl</u>, <u>I immediately recognized her</u>.
         subordinate clause   principal clause

What is the conjunction joining these two clauses? What makes them both clauses?

In each of the above examples, the main clauses are those that can stand by themselves as complete sentences. The subordinate clauses all depend for their meaning on the principal clauses and hence cannot stand alone.

Notice that all subordinate clauses begin with either a subordinate conjunction (Module 6) or a relative pronoun—also known as a "conjunctive pronoun." The relative pronoun often functions as the subject of its clause.

EXERCISE 8.1.1

In the sentences below, underline the principal clause once and the subordinate clause twice.

1. He went to sleep after the guests had left.

2. Before he ate breakfast, he went for a jog.

3. A woman, whom I knew from school, was struck by a car yesterday.

4. If you enjoy apples, you should read about the MacIntoshes.

5. Since the party was over, we drove to Rasha's house where there was another party in progress.

8.2   KINDS OF SUBORDINATE CLAUSES

There are several kinds of subordinate clauses:

1. adjective clauses (restrictive and nonrestrictive)

2. adverb clauses

3. noun clauses

ADJECTIVE CLAUSES

The **adjective clause** functions as a single adjective. It describes or modifies a noun or pronoun. Adjective clauses usually begin with a conjunction that is also a relative pronoun. Examples are *who*, *which*, and *that*. They are sometimes referred to as *relative clauses*. (See Module 2 for a further discussion of relative pronouns.)

■ **Example:**

The flowers <u>that grow there</u> are beautiful.

In this sentence, *that grow there* is a subordinate adjectival (or relative) clause. It begins with the relative pronoun *that* and modifies the noun *flowers*. Notice that the main clause in this sentence is interrupted: *The flowers ... are beautiful.* Such interruptions occur frequently with adjective clauses.

Restrictive Adjective Clauses

A **restrictive clause** provides information about a noun or pronoun that is necessary to complete a thought. Commas do not separate a restrictive clause from the rest of its sentence because it cannot be left out of the sentence without changing the meaning.

■ **Example:**

Salespeople <u>who are on the road by 8:30 A.M.</u> will make their quotas.

Who are on the road by 8:30 A.M. is a restrictive adjective clause because it provides information that is necessary to complete the meaning of the sentence. The sentence does not mean that *all* salespeople will make their quotas. It means that only salespeople who are on the road by 8:30 A.M. will make their quotas.

Nonrestrictive Clauses

A **nonrestrictive clause** is an adjective clause that provides additional information about the noun it modifies. This type of clause is not needed to complete the sense of the sentence in which it appears. Commas must precede and follow a nonrestrictive clause.

■ **Example:**

> Carol, <u>who is a college graduate</u>, cannot get a job.

Who is a college graduate is an adjective clause because it modifies the noun *Carol*. Since the information it gives us about Carol is not necessary for the reader to understand the meaning of the sentence, it is also a nonrestrictive adjective clause. Since the information is not essential, it must be set off by commas.

In the following sentences, the adjective clause is underlined and has been labelled as either restrictive or nonrestrictive.

> 1. Our horse Dobbin, <u>which was old and tired</u>, served us well. [nonrestrictive]

The adjective clause *which was old and tired* is nonrestrictive because it is not essential to the meaning of the sentence. If the clause were left out, the sentence would still make sense: "Our horse Dobbin served us well."

> 2. People <u>who live in glass houses</u> should not throw stones. [restrictive]

The adjective clause *who live in glass houses* is restrictive because it is essential to the meaning of the sentence. If the clause were left out, it would completely change the meaning of the sentence: "People should not throw stones." Note that the essential clause has no punctuation around it.

> 3. Yumin, <u>who works in our office</u>, typed five letters. [nonrestrictive]

The adjective clause *who works in our office* is nonrestrictive because it is not essential to the meaning of the sentence. If the clause were left out, the sentence would still make sense: "Yumin typed five letters." *Who works in our office* provides additional information about the subject *Yumin*.

> 4. Mohammed, <u>who lives next door</u>, was in an accident. [nonrestrictive]

The adjective clause *who lives next door* is nonestrictive because it is not essential to the meaning of the sentence. If the clause were left out, the sentence would still make sense: "Mohammed was in an accident." *Who lives next door* simply gives the reader additional information about the subject, *Mohammed*.

> 5. People <u>who love cats</u> are generally very friendly. [restrictive]

The adjective clause *who love cats* is restrictive because it is essential to the meaning of the sentence. We are not just talking about people in general. We are talking specifically about people who love cats; therefore, it is essential to have the restrictive clause. If the clause were left out, it would completely change the meaning of the sentence: "People are generally very friendly."

In each of the above examples, the adjective clauses modify a noun. The non-restrictive adjective clauses provide information not essential to the meaning of the sentence. They are separated from the rest of the sentence by commas. The restrictive adjective clauses are *not* separated from the rest of the sentence by commas because they provide information essential to the meaning of the sentence in which they appear.

> The novel <u>that I brought to school</u> is on the desk. [restrictive]

> The novel, *The Wars*, <u>which was written by Timothy Findley</u>, is on the table. [nonrestrictive]

In most cases, when a relative clause modifies a common noun, it is restrictive; when it modifies a proper noun, it is nonrestrictive.

ADVERB CLAUSES

An **adverb clause** functions as a single adverb. It describes or modifies a verb, an adjective, or another adverb in a given sentence. Adverb clauses begin with subordinate conjunctions (see Module 6) rather than relative pronouns (see Module 2). Ask the following questions of the verb or adjective or adverb the clause seems to be modifying: how?, when?, where?, or why? If you get an answer to any of these questions, the subordinate clause in the given sentence will be functioning as an adverb. It will also modify the questioned word.

■ **Examples:**

> Frank went to the store <u>before it closed</u>.

Before it closed is a subordinate adverb clause. It begins with the subordinate conjunction *before*, and is followed by the subject pronoun *it* and the verb *closed*. How did we find and designate it as adverb? We turned to the verb *went* and asked the question "when?" The answer is *before it closed*.

> Rina is wise <u>because she has read many books</u>.

Because she has read many books is a subordinate adverb clause. It begins with the subordinate conjunction *because*, and is followed by the subject pronoun *she* and the verb *is*. How did we find and designate it as an adverb? We turned to the adjective *wise* and asked the question "why?" The answer is *because she reads many books*.

NOTE: When a subordinate clause starts a sentence, it is followed by a comma.

EXERCISE 8.2.1

In the following sentences, the adverb clauses are underlined. For each one of these clauses, state what question is asked of what word (to inform you that these clauses are indeed adverbs). Also, give the part of speech of each of the modified words.

■ **Example:**

> <u>When she was ready</u>, she took the plunge.

Question Asked	Of What Word	Part of Speech
when?	took	verb

1. Sue left school <u>before I arrived</u>.

Question Asked	Of What Word	Part of Speech

2. He loved the forest <u>because it was beautiful</u>.

Question Asked	Of What Word	Part of Speech

3. She buried the treasure <u>where it would never be found</u>.

Question Asked	Of What Word	Part of Speech

4. The document is important <u>because it is very old</u>.

Question Asked	Of What Word	Part of Speech

5. <u>While it was raining</u>, the men took cover.

Question Asked	Of What Word	Part of Speech

HIDDEN SUBORDINATE CLAUSES

Because of an ellipsis (omission), some subordinate clauses are said to be "hidden." This makes them a little difficult to identify.

Look at a few subordinate clauses that contain elliptical (omitted) words. Even though words are omitted, they are *understood to be present*. Consider the following sentences written first with omitted word(s), and then with the omitted word(s) added.

a) He said he would come.

He said <u>that</u> he would come.

b) I am older than he.

I am older than he <u>is old</u>.

c) I knew Kimo better than him.

I knew Kimo better than <u>I knew</u> him.

In this example, we require *him* to be object of the elliptical verb *knew*.

> d) I knew Kimo better than he.
>   I knew Kimo better than he <u>knew Kimo</u>.

In this example, we require *he* to be subject of the elliptical verb *knew*.

> e) While still a toddler, my father coached me.
>   While <u>I was</u> still a toddler, my father coached me.

Ellipsis is permissible only when the subjects of both the subordinate and the principal clauses are the same. In the elliptical version of this example, the elliptical subject is the understood "I." The subject of the main clause is *father*. As the subjects are not the same, the meaning is incorrect, and therefore the ellipsis is not permissible.

From the above examples, we can see that subordinate clauses are sometimes hidden because of omitted words. Be aware of these ellipses when you are analyzing sentence clauses.

EXERCISE 8.2.2

Rewrite the following sentences by inserting the missing ellipses. Then give the relationship of each elliptical clause.

1. Janet said she would be present at the meeting.

   _____

   _____

2. While walking to the cinema with my father, I told him an interesting story.

   _____

   _____

3. Meredith likes Thomas better than him.

   _____

   _____

4. Weng-fook admires Jeannette more than he.

   _____

   _____

5. When passing the courthouse together, we were caught in a sudden rainstorm.

   _____

   _____

EXERCISE 8.2.3

Correct the hidden clause in the following sentences. In sentence form, give a reason for each correction.

1. He sings better than me.

_____

_____

2. No person could be sloppier than her.

_____

_____

3. You say Elena is more intelligent than whom?

_____

_____

4. Whose moral standards are higher than his?

_____

_____

5. She is a better athlete than his.

_____

_____

NOUN CLAUSES

A **noun clause** functions as a single noun in a sentence. As such, it may be:

      a) subject of a verb

      b) object of a verb

      c) object of a preposition, or

      d) subjective completion (complement)

A noun clause is often introduced by a subordinate conjunction (see Module 6) such as *that, what, when, where, whether,* and *why.*

■ **Examples:**

1. <u>That the earth is round</u> is a fact.

That the earth is round is a noun clause. It functions as the noun subject of the second verb *is*. Note that the subordinate conjunction introducing the clause is *That*.

2. <u>When you do it</u> is no concern of mine.

When you do it is a noun clause. It functions as the noun subject of the verb *is*. The subordinate conjunction introducing the clause is *When*.

3. <u>Where you go</u> does not concern me.

Where you go is a noun clause, subject of the verb phrase *does not concern*. The introductory conjunction is *Where*.

4. <u>Whether I said it or not</u> is not the point here.

Whether I said it or not is a noun clause, subject of the verb *is*. The introductory conjunction is *Whether*.

5. He asked <u>what I was doing</u>.

What I was doing is a noun clause, object of the verb *asked*, and it is introduced by the conjunction *what*.

Earlier we noted that a main clause can always stand alone as a complete thought because it must contain both a subject and a verb and must make sense. At that time we stated that a noun clause was an exception to that rule. It is now time to discuss this exception further.

In the following sentences, the noun clauses are underlined. Following each, its relationship is stated.

1. <u>Where he found the treasure</u> is a secret. [subject of the verb *is*]

2. <u>When the accident occurred</u> is not known. [subject of the verb phrase *is known*]

These two examples are not simple sentences. They are complex sentences. In both examples, the subject of the verb in the main clause is an entire noun clause. Note that these noun clauses are necessary for the sentences to make sense. Thus, in these examples, the entire sentence is the main clause. Put another way, the main clause cannot stand on its own because the subordinate noun clause is also the subject of the main clause.

Now observe the following examples:

3. Her brother knew <u>where he had gone</u>. [object of the verb *knew*; answers the question "what?" directed to the verb]

4. We wondered <u>why the baby was crying</u>. [object of the verb *wondered*; answers the question "what?" directed to the verb]

5. My uncle knows <u>where the strawberries grow</u>. [object of the verb *knows*; answers the question "what?" directed to the verb]

We have seen that to find adverb clauses we ask the questions "how?", "when?", "where?", and "why?" To find the objects of verbs and prepositions we ask the verb or the preposition "what?" (things) or "whom?" (persons).

Noun Clause Relationships

One must discover the relationship of noun clauses in sentences in order to know how they are being used in those sentences. For example, are they functioning as subject of a verb, object of a verb, object of a preposition, or as a subjective completion (complement)? Noun clauses cannot function as indirect objects.

As noted above, one finds objects (whether they are single words, phrases, or clauses) by asking verbs or prepositions the question "what?" The answer will be the "object."

> *NOTE:* Now that you have studied words, phrases, and clauses, a general principle should have emerged: the different parts of speech perform the functions allotted to them.
>
> *Nouns* function as subjects of verbs, objects of verbs, objects of prepositions, and subjective completions (complements).
>
> *Adjectives* function as modifiers of nouns and pronouns.
>
> *Adverbs* function as modifiers of verbs, adjectives, or other adverbs.
>
> The point is that it does not matter whether you use a single-word noun, a noun phrase, or a noun clause. If the word, phrase, or clause is performing the function of a noun, it will have noun value. Phrases and clauses as parts of speech must be thought of as single units. The same point applies equally to both adjectives and adverbs.

EXERCISE 8.2.4

For each of the following sentences, write a sentence in which you:

a) identify the subordinate clause, and

b) state their relationship to other elements in the sentence.

■ **Examples:**

a) I like people <u>who are punctual</u>.

Who are punctual is a restrictive subordinate adjective clause that modifies the noun *people*.

b) <u>While he was talking</u>, the telephone rang.

While he was talking is a subordinate adverbial clause that modifies the verb *rang*.

How did we get these solutions? First, we identified the subordinate clause. Next, we identified the kind of subordinate clause. Then we identified the relationship of the clause in its sentence. Finally, we used full sentences to present our answers.

1. I heard that you went on a trip.

_____

_____

2. We were not fooled by what you said.

_____

_____

3. Where they sat in the stadium was protected from the rain.

_____

_____

4. The fact that I had been sick did not influence their decision.

_____

_____

_____

5. My locker is where I keep my books.

_____

_____

_____

EXERCISE 8.2.5

Underline the subordinate clauses and identify the kind of clause.

1. The woman who wrote this letter shows remarkable humour.

   Kind of clause:

   _____

2. Because we had a reservation, we were seated immediately.

   Kind of clause:

   _____

3. What the coach says is important to the team.

   Kind of clause:

   _____

4. You watch the movie while I make the popcorn.

   Kind of clause:

   _____

5. John McIntosh, who was a United Empire Loyalist, came to Upper Canada in 1796.

Kind of clause:

_____

EXERCISE 8.2.6

Specify the kind and relationship of the subordinate clauses in the sentences below.

1. Chi stayed until the work was finished.

Kind of clause:

_____

Relationship:

_____

2. Susan returned the wallet she found at the bus stop.

Kind of clause.

_____

Relationship:

_____

3. The pond is where we like to swim.

Kind of clause:

_____

Relationship:

_____

4. I heard you got a new job.

Kind of clause:

_____

Relationship:

_____

5. What is in the box is a mystery.

Kind of clause:

_____

Relationship:

_____

EXERCISE 8.2.7

In the following sentences, underline the subordinate clauses. Circle the word to which each clause is related.

1. The party became lively after George and Carol arrived.

2. Why he became a politician was explained in his book.

3. The old house was bigger than she remembered.

4. The arsonist who started the fire has never been caught.

5. She is the driver of the car that hit me.

EXERCISE 8.2.8

In the sentences below, underline each subordinate clause (some are hidden). Identify each as an adjective (restrictive or nonrestrictive), adverb, or noun. State the word to which each is related.

1. The college counselling centre offers help to anyone who needs it.

   Kind of clause:

   _____

   Related to the word:

   _____

2. My adviser suggested I enrol in a special course.

   Kind of clause:

   _____

   Related to the word:

   _____

3. I well recall the day I won the speech contest.

   Kind of clause:

   _____

   Related to the word:

   _____

4. I looked for the book that I had seen on Liyu's desk.

   Kind of clause:

   _____

   Related to the word:

   _____

5. Rob told them while they were eating dinner.

Kind of clause:

_____

Related to the word:

_____

EXERCISE 8.2.9

Add the indicated subordinate clause to the main clause to complete the sentences below.

1. (adverb clause) Han-Ngar won the race.

_____

_____

2. (adjective clause) The customer seemed to be arguing with the bank teller.

_____

_____

3. (adjective clause) The cat walked into the living room and jumped onto the window ledge.

_____

_____

4. (adverb clause) I keep my valuables in a locked cabinet.

_____

_____

5. (adjective clause) The Solomons painted the house.

_____

_____

EXERCISE 8.2.10

In the following sentences, underline the subordinate clauses. Using sentences, state the kind and relationship of each.

1. What he wanted us to do for him seemed utterly impossible.

   Kind of clause:

   _____

   Relationship:

   _____

2. We visited the area where gold had first been discovered.

   Kind of clause:

   _____

   Relationship:

   _____

3. Do not complete the rest of the form until you have seen your adviser.

   Kind of clause:

   _____

   Relationship:

   _____

4. Plato argued that artists should be censored.

   Kind of clause:

   _____

   Relationship:

   _____

5. I cannot go with you today because I have to go to the dentist.

   Kind of clause:

   _____

   Relationship:

   _____

EXERCISE 8.2.11

Write sentences according to the instructions given.

1. "While I waited for a bus" as an adverb clause modifying a verb.

_____

_____

_____

2. "That I'll be trapped in an elevator" as a noun clause subject of a verb.

_____

_____

_____

3. "That I should come to this" as an adverb clause modifying an adjective.

_____

_____

_____

4. "Whoever holds the lucky number" as a noun clause object of a preposition.

_____

_____

_____

5. "That the journey would take ten years" as a noun clause used as object of a verb.

_____

_____

_____

8.3   TYPES OF SENTENCES

Sentences will be discussed in detail in Module 9. But since sentences consist of clauses, you should know about these now.

SIMPLE SENTENCES

Simple sentences contain *only one clause* (a group of words containing both a subject and a verb). That one clause must be independent and thus must express a complete thought. However, if you used only simple sentences, your writing would be monotonous, jerky, and simplistic. It is now time, therefore, to learn how to write more elaborate sentences in order to obtain a more mature style. This can be done by varying your clausal structure as outlined below.

COMPOUND SENTENCES

A **compound sentence** is made up of two or more main clauses. Each of these clauses is independent, is a complete thought, and makes sense by itself. Moreover, *each clause is of equal importance in the sentence*. Note also that there are no subordinate clauses in a compound sentence.

To combine two or more main clauses, you may use one of three methods:

1. Use a coordinate conjunction (*and*, *or*, *but*) (see Module 6) preceded by a comma.

■ **Example:**

> We heard the train, but we did not see it.

We heard the train—main clause

we did not see it—main clause

Each of these statements can stand by itself as a complete thought.

but—coordinate conjunction preceded by a comma

This is the linking word between the two main clauses.

2. Use a semicolon (;) in place of a coordinate conjunction. (See Module 10, "Punctuation.")

■ **Example:**

> We heard the train; we did not see it.

We heard the train—main clause

we did not see it—a second, closely related main clause.

Each of these statements is independent. But since they are closely related, they can be linked by a semicolon.

3. Use a semicolon (see Module 10) and a transitional word or phrase followed by a comma. Transitional words are good bridges and are usually good at indicating a relationship.

■ **Example:**

We heard the train; <u>however</u>, we did not see it.

We heard the train—main clause

we did not see it—main clause

; however,—a semicolon, a transitional word, and a comma combine the two clauses. The omitted coordinate conjunction *but* is replaced by a semicolon.

Do not confuse transitional words and phrases with coordinate or subordinate conjunctions. Some of the most common transitional words and phrases are listed below:

also	for example	however	otherwise
as a result	for instance	instead	therefore
consequently	furthermore	meanwhile	thus
finally	hence	moreover	yet

Each of the above will be preceded by a semicolon (;) and followed by a comma (,).

In the following sentences, each method discussed above is used to combine the main clauses.

1. The sky became dark. It did not snow.

Two main clauses are isolated as separate sentences.

The sky became dark, but it did not snow.

Two main clauses are linked by the coordinate conjunction *but*.

The sky became dark; it did not snow.

A semicolon is used to link two closely related main clauses.

The sky became dark; however, it did not snow.

A semicolon and a transitional word have been used to link the two closely related main clauses. Notice the use of a comma following the transitional word. Note also that you have four choices. This will help give you variety in your sentence structure.

2. Carol entered the haunted house. She was very afraid.

Carol entered the haunted house, and she was very afraid.

Carol entered the haunted house; she was very afraid.

Carol entered the haunted house; hence, she was very afraid.

... thus, she was very afraid.

... therefore, she was very afraid.

In these examples, we were able to combine two main clauses into a compound sentence. Instead of writing two simple sentences, which would have been monotonous, we were able to write compound sentences that are tighter or neater in style.

EXERCISE 8.3.1

Combine the following main clauses into compound sentences. Where applicable, replace the repeated nouns with pronouns. Vary your combinations by using all three methods you have been taught.

1. Natsunor wanted to go to the movies. Natsunor did not want to go alone.

   _____

   _____

2. Chris bought some land in Minden. Chris built a cottage on it.

   _____

   _____

3. The water seemed warm. The water was too cold for swimming.

   _____

   _____

4. The boys went fishing. The boys did not catch anything.

   _____

   _____

5. It was cold. They did not mind.

   _____

   _____

COMPLEX SENTENCES

A **complex sentence** combines only one main clause with one or more subordinate clauses (see Module 9). In a complex sentence, the subordinate clause may occur at different points in the sentence. For example:

1. Before a main clause:

   <u>After he left the party</u>, Frank went straight home.

2. After a main clause:

   I read this book <u>because it was assigned in class</u>.

3. Interrupting a main clause:

People <u>who are friendly</u> are the most popular at a party.

4. Before and after a main clause:

<u>When the band took the stage</u>, they played a song <u>that was on their new compact disc</u>.

NOTE: In Example 4 there is only one main clause, but there are two subordinate clauses.

For the correct punctuation of these sentences, see Module 10.

COMPOUND-COMPLEX SENTENCES

A sentence made up of two or more main clauses and one or more subordinate clauses is called a **compound-complex sentence**. (See Module 9, "Sentences.")

■ **Example:**

The farmer planted his corn early, but it did not grow very well because there was too much rain that summer.

The farmer planted his corn early is the first main clause.

but is a coordinate conjunction.

it did not grow very well is the second main clause.

because is a subordinate conjunction.

there was too much rain that summer is a subordinate clause.

EXERCISE 8.3.2

In the following sentences,

a) identify the types of conjunctions used (see Module 6),

b) identify the sentences as compound, complex, or compound-complex.

1. He will do it unless he is too busy.

Type of conjunction:

_____

Type of sentence:

_____

2. They did not have a map, but they had no trouble getting there.

Type of conjunction:

_____

Type of sentence:

_____

3. When I was on vacation, all of my plants died because they were not watered.

   Type of conjunction:

   _____

   Type of sentence:

   _____

4. Susan walked slowly because the sidewalks were icy.

   Type of conjunction:

   _____

   Type of sentence:

   _____

5. Santo wanted to go to the concert, but he did not have enough money for the tickets.

   Type of conjunction:

   _____

   Type of sentence:

   _____

EXERCISE 8.3.3

In the following sentences, underline the main clause(s) once and the subordinate clause(s) twice. Indicate if the sentences are compound, complex, or compound-complex.

1. Carol hoped to see the man whom she had met at the party last week, but he was not there.

   Kind of sentence:

   _____

2. Before Masoud arrived, the band had started to play.

   Kind of sentence:

   _____

3. The cake had been beautifully decorated, but Anne tripped and dropped it on the floor.

   Kind of sentence:

   _____

4. After the train left the station, the porter came to collect the tickets.

   Kind of sentence:

   _____

5. The young boy opened his present; inside he found a puppy.

   Kind of sentence:

   _____

EXERCISE 8.3.4

Write a sentence according to the instructions below.

1. a compound sentence using *but* as a coordinate conjunction

   _____

   _____

2. a complex sentence using *because* as a conjunction

   _____

   _____

3. a compound sentence using the transitional word *however*

   _____

   _____

4. a compound-complex sentence using the coordinate conjunction *but* and the subordinate conjunction *after*

   _____

   _____

5. a compound-complex sentence using the coordinate conjunction *and* as well as the subordinate conjunction (relative pronoun) *that*

   _____

   _____

ANSWER KEY

EXERCISE 8.1.1

1. He went to sleep after the guests had left.
3. A woman, whom I knew from school, was struck by a car yesterday.
5. Since the party was over, we drove to Fred's house where there was another party in progress.

EXERCISE 8.2.1

Question Asked	Of What Word	Part of Speech
1. when?	left	verb
3. where?	buried	verb
5. when?	took	verb

EXERCISE 8.2.2

1. Janet said (*that*) she would be present at the meeting.
   object of the verb *said*
3. Meredith likes Thomas better than (*she likes*) him.
   modifies the adverb *better*
5. When (*we were*) passing the courthouse together, we were caught in a sudden rainstorm.
   modifies the verb phrase *were caught*

EXERCISE 8.2.3

1. He sings better than *I*.
   The pronoun *I* is required in the subjective case to be subject of the understood verb *sing*.
3. You say Elena is more intelligent than *who*?
   The pronoun *who* is required in the subjective case to be subject of the understood verb *is*.
5. She is a better athlete than *he*.
   The pronoun *he* is required in the subjective case to be subject of the understood verb *is*.

EXERCISE 8.2.4

1. The clause *that you went on a trip* is a noun clause that is object of the verb *heard.*
3. The clause *where they sat in the audience* is a noun clause that is subject of the verb *was protected.*
5. *Where I keep my boots* is a noun clause and it is the subjective completion of the linking verb *is.*

EXERCISE 8.2.5

1. The woman who wrote this letter shows remarkable humour.
   Restrictive adjective
3. What the coach says is important to the team.
   Noun
5. John McIntosh, who was a United Empire Loyalist, came to Upper Canada in 1796.
   Nonrestrictive adjective

EXERCISE 8.2.6

    1. adverb, modifies the verb *stayed*
    3. noun, subjective completion of the verb *is*
    5. noun, subject of the verb *is*

EXERCISE 8.2.7

    1. The party became lively after George and Carol arrived.

    3. The old house was bigger than she remembered.

    5. She is the driver of the car that hit me.

EXERCISE 8.2.8

    1. The college counselling centre offers help to anyone who needs it.
       Kind of clause: restrictive adjective
       Related to the word: *anyone*
    3. I well recall the day (that) I won the speech contest.
       Kind of clause: restrictive adjective
       Related to the word: *day*
    5. Rob told them while they were eating dinner.
       Kind of clause: adverb
       Related to the word: *told*

EXERCISE 8.2.9

Answers will vary.

EXERCISE 8.2.10

    1. What he wanted us to do for him seemed utterly impossible.
       noun, subject of the verb *seemed*
    3. Do not complete the rest of the form until you have seen your adviser.
       adverb, modifies the verb phrase *do complete*
    5. I cannot go with you today because I have to go to the dentist.
       adverb, modifies the verb phrase *can go*

EXERCISE 8.2.11

Answers will vary.

EXERCISE 8.3.1

Answers will vary.
    1. Natsunor wanted to go to the movies, but she did not want to go alone.
    3. The water seemed warm, but it was too cold for swimming.
    5. It was cold, but they did not seem to mind.

EXERCISE 8.3.2

    1. adverb, complex
    3. adverb, compound-complex
    5. coordinate, compound

EXERCISE 8.3.3

    1. Carol hoped to see the man whom she had met at the party last week, but he was not there.
       Kind of sentence: compound-complex

3. <u>The cake was beautifully decorated</u>, but <u>Anne tripped and dropped it on the floor.</u>
   Kind of sentence: compound
5. <u>The young boy opened his present</u>; <u>inside he found a puppy</u>.
   Kind of sentence: compound

EXERCISE 8.3.4

Answers will vary.

MODULE 9

SENTENCES

Learning Outcome Statement

By successfully completing a series of module exercises, you will be able to:

1. recognize sentences and thus minimize major errors in grammar and in compositional style;

2. apply variety to sentence structure to maximize writing style and minimize boredom by:

   a) varying word order,

   b) using different types of sentences according to purpose (declarative, interrogative, imperative, exclamatory),

   c) using different types of sentences according to grammatical structure (simple, compound, complex, compound-complex),

   d) selecting different formats (natural, inverted, and split), and

   e) using modifiers.

SENTENCES

9.1 WHAT IS A SENTENCE?

A **sentence** consists of a group of words that must contain a subject and a verb. It must also express a complete thought. (For further elaboration, see Modules 3, 7, and 8.)

The verb, excluding its modifiers, can be referred to as the **bare predicate**. The subject, excluding modifiers, can be referred to as the **bare subject**.

A sentence has two major parts: complete subject and complete predicate. The **complete subject** will consist of a noun or pronoun (the person or thing about which the writer is making a statement—see Modules 1 and 2), together with any of its adjectival modifiers (words that limit or describe the subject noun—see Module 4). The **complete predicate** will consist of a verb (the action or linking word that tells what the subject is doing—see Module 3), together with its adverbial modifiers (see Module 4).

■ **Examples:**

In the following sentences, the bare subject is underlined once; the bare predicate (verb) twice:

> 1. The <u>children</u> <u>are playing</u> in the school yard.

The bare subject of this sentence is *children*, as they are the ones doing the action. *Are playing* is the bare predicate, or verb phrase, of the sentence, as it states what the children are doing.

> 2. <u>We</u> <u>went</u> dancing last night.

The bare subject of this sentence is *we*, as we were the ones doing the action. *Went* is the bare predicate of the sentence, which states what we did.

> 3. A <u>school</u> <u>is, or should be</u>, an institution of learning.

The bare subject of this sentence is *school* as it is the thing being talked about. *Is, or should be* is the bare predicate of the sentence.

In the following sentences, the complete subject is underlined once; the complete predicate twice:

> 1. <u>I</u> <u>enjoy most sports</u>.

I is both the complete subject, and the bare subject, as the subject *I* has no modifiers in this sentence. *Enjoy most sports* is the complete predicate, which includes the bare predicate *enjoy* and its object *most sports*.

> 2. <u>Do</u> <u>you</u>?

You is the complete subject and *do* is the complete predicate, as there are no modifiers in this sentence.

> 3. <u>At school</u> <u>we</u> <u>learn many things</u>.

We is the complete subject of this sentence, with no modifiers. *At school* and *learn many things* make up the complete predicate, with *learn* as the bare predicate and *at school* and *many things* being modifiers of the bare predicate.

4. <u>Usually by February</u> <u>people</u> <u>long for spring</u>.

People is the complete subject of this sentence because, the subject, *people* has no modifiers. The rest of the sentence makes up the complete predicate. *Long* is the bare predicate. *For spring* and *usually by February* are modifiers of the bare predicate.

EXERCISE 9.1.1

In the following sentences underline all bare subjects once and all bare predicates twice. In complete sentences, explain your decision in the space provided.

■ **Example:**

Many <u>people</u> <u>work</u> hard every day.

People is the bare subject, as they are the ones we are talking about. *Work,* the verb, is the bare predicate of the sentence because this is the action that the bare subject is doing.

> *NOTE:* If a subject happens to be *you* understood, write in the *you*.

1. Kumar went to the ballet twice last week.

_____

_____

2. Incidentally, roses are now blooming in Picardy.

_____

_____

3. Go to the corner store for some Lifesavers.

_____

_____

4. Are you happy with your lot in life?

_____

_____

5. Sit up straight in your seat, Darin.

_____

_____

EXERCISE 9.1.2

In the following sentences, underline all complete subjects once, and all complete predicates twice. In full sentences, explain your decision.

■ **Example:**

<u>Occasionally I</u> <u>go for long walks in the country</u>.

I is the complete subject of the sentence. *Go* is the bare predicate of the sentence indicating the action of the subject, with *for long walks in the country* and *occasionally* as modifiers of the bare predicate.

1. Occasionally, Dr. Ramjeet's class is taken out into the country to study nature.

_____

_____

2. Are the people of Cuba happy with Fidel Castro as their dictator?

_____

_____

3. Do you speak Greek, or any other language besides English?

_____

_____

4. The baseball team at our school is, we think, about to win the championship.

_____

_____

5. Do you ever wonder what it would be like to live on the moon?

_____

_____

9.2 PURPOSE

Sentences can serve different purposes. They can be used to make a statement, to ask a question, to give an order or command, or to make a statement of emphasis or strong emotion. There are four kinds of sentences: assertive, interrogative, imperative, and exclamatory.

■ **Examples:**

1. An **assertive** sentence makes a statement. It is also known as a **declarative** sentence.

> I am going home.
>
> You were absent yesterday.
>
> In the spring, more people go outside.
>
> Usually, when people are in good health, they experience a sense of well-being.

2. An **interrogative** sentence asks a question. It always ends with a question mark (?).

> Have you done your homework?
>
> Are your parents well?
>
> Do you want to vote for the Liberal party?
>
> When you come home from work, what is the first thing that you do?

3. An **imperative** sentence gives an order or command. The subject in this type of sentence is assumed.

> Do as I say.
>
> Wake up early and get out into the fresh air.
>
> Never tell lies; always be honest.
>
> Sit down and be quiet.

4. An **exclamatory** sentence expresses strong emotion. It usually ends with an exclamation mark (!) (see Module 10).

> What a beautiful day!
>
> How wonderful are my friends!
>
> Help! Our house is on fire!

EXERCISE 9.2.1

State in a single word whether the following sentences are assertive, interrogative, imperative, or exclamatory. Explain your answer in complete sentences.

1. What did you say?

_____

_____

_____

2. Look carefully to both left and right when you cross the road.

_____

_____

_____

3. If you look carefully whenever you cross the street, you should always be safe.

_____

_____

_____

4. Nothing succeeds like success!

_____

_____

_____

5. While driving back home late at night, we were caught in a blizzard.

_____

_____

_____

9.3 CLAUSAL STRUCTURE

You have already learned to recognize and define sentences according to their purpose—for example, assertive, interrogative, imperative, and exclamatory. There is another way to get variety in sentence structure. This involves writing sentences according to clausal structure (see Module 8 for more information on clauses).

1. A **simple** sentence expresses one complete thought and contains only one subject and one verb.

    a) Go home!

    b) I am in the garden.

    c) At the office, I work hard daily.

    d) What are you doing tonight?

    e) Nothing is so rare as a day in June!

A simple sentence may be imperative (a), assertive (b, c), interrogative (d), or exclamatory (e).

2. A **compound** sentence expresses two or more complete thoughts, and contains two or more main verbs. Therefore, it is made up of two or more main clauses.

    We are cousins, and we are both married. (two main clauses)

    OR

    We are cousins; we are also both married.

    You are intelligent, and you are also charitable. (two main clauses)

    OR

    You are intelligent; you are also charitable.

    I came, I saw, I conquered. (3 main clauses)

3. A **complex** sentence expresses only one complete thought and at least one incomplete thought. Put another way, a complex sentence must contain only one main clause and at least one subordinate clause. Refer to Module 8 for a discussion of clauses.

            subordinate clause   main clause
    a) [When I come home from work], [I am usually tired].

                   main clause   subordinate clause
    b) [Crocuses, tulips, and daffodils reminded me] [that it was spring].

            subordinate clause   main clause
    c) [When I think of my past], [I am grateful to my parents], [who
            subordinate clause
    gave me the gift of education].

              subordinate clause   main clause
    d) [Because I love listening to classical music], [I often turn on my
                  subordinate clause
    car radio] [so that I can enjoy the music of the so-called three B's
    —Bach, Beethoven, and Brahms].

NOTE: If the coordinating conjunction (for example, *and*, *but*) is present, a comma will precede it; if the conjunction is omitted between two complete thoughts, it will be replaced by a semicolon. (See Module 10, "Punctuation.")

4. A **compound-complex** sentence contains two or more complete thoughts and one or more incomplete thoughts. Put another way, a compound-complex sentence must contain at least two main clauses and at least one subordinate clause.

Ms. Rashid is my teacher, and I admire her, especially when she helps me with my homework.

OR

Ms. Rashid is my teacher; I especially admire her when she helps me with my homework.

I go for long walks when the sky is blue, but I stay in by the fire when the sky is grey.

OR

I go for long walks when the sky is blue; I stay in by the fire when the sky is grey.

If you come to visit this evening when dinner is over, I shall be able to spend some time with you; I shall also be able to help you with your problem.

Our collie dog is a joy to watch because he is always doing tricks, and children shout with joy when they see him do somersaults.

OR

Our collie dog is a joy to watch because he is always doing tricks; children shout with joy when they see him do somersaults.

A varied use of simple, compound, complex, and compound-complex sentences will produce variety by having a mix of long, medium, and short sentences, and will avoid a monotonous and jerky style of writing.

EXERCISE 9.3.1

In a sentence, state whether the following sentences are simple, compound, complex, or compound-complex. Explain your decision.

1. If you do what I ask, you will not be disappointed.

_____

_____

2. Get to work!

_____

_____

3. I am ready now to do what you say I should.

_____

_____

4. I went to the gym and I spoke to my coach.

_____

_____

5. As he was my friend, I liked him; as he was my teacher, I respected him!

_____

_____

9.4 WORD ORDER

The natural word order in English is: subject and subject modifiers, followed by the verb and its modifiers, followed by the object of the verb and the object's modifiers.

The natural word order, however, can be changed for variety, thus adding more interest to your writing. There are two other ways of achieving variety: inverted format and split format.

NATURAL FORMAT

Every one of these five sample sentences begins with a subject and its modifiers, followed by a verb and its modifiers. This is the natural word order.

■ **Examples:**

The arthritic cat hobbled painfully across the carpet.

Cat is the bare subject of the sentence, modified by *the* and *arthritic* in order to make the complete subject. *Hobbled* is the bare predicate, modified by *painfully* and *across the carpet* in order to make the complete predicate.

The old man laughed heartily at his own joke.

Man is the bare subject of the sentence, modified by *the* and *old* in order to make the complete subject. *Laughed* is the bare predicate, modified by *heartily* and *at his own joke* in order to make the complete predicate.

A tree in our backyard is loaded with red apples.

Tree is the bare subject of the sentence, modified by *a* and *in our backyard* in order to make the complete subject. *Is* is the bare predicate, modified by *loaded* and *with red apples* in order to make the complete predicate.

The Toronto Maple Leafs hockey team assembled on the outdoor rink for a practice skate.

Team is the bare subject of the sentence, modified by *hockey* and *The Toronto Maple Leafs* in order to make the complete subject. *Assembled* is the bare predicate, modified by *on the outdoor rink* and *for a practice skate* in order to make the complete predicate.

The tiny, crying baby wanted to be lifted from his crib.

Baby is the bare subject of the sentence, modified by *the*, *tiny*, and *crying* in order to make the complete subject. *Wanted* is the bare predicate, modified by *to be lifted from his crib* in order to make the complete predicate.

INVERTED FORMAT

This format inverts or reverses the order of the subject and the verb. This occurs in sentences beginning with *There is*, *There are*, *Here is*, *Here are*, and in sentences beginning with *How*, *When*, *Where*, *Why*, or, *What*. In all of these examples, the subject comes *after* the verb. The inverted order is also used in simple questions that use the verb *to be*.

■ **Examples:** (subject is underlined)

There is a <u>book</u> on the table.

In natural order (subject first), this sentence would read: *A book is there on the table*. As you can see, the subject and verb are reversed, but the meaning is still the same.

There are <u>seven e's</u> in this sentence.

The natural format of this sentence would read: *Seven e's are there in this sentence*. Again, the subject and verb are reversed, but the meaning is still the same.

Here is <u>my resignation</u>.

The natural format of this sentence would read: *My resignation is here*. The meaning is still the same.

Here are <u>my credentials</u>.

Again, the natural format would read: *My credentials are here*. Again, the meaning is still the same.

Are <u>you</u> ill?

The natural format would read: *You are ill*. Convert the question into a statement to get the natural format.

> *NOTE:* The subject is the person, thing, or idea about which a statement is being made.

SPLIT FORMAT

In split format words come between the subject and the verb. Although the verb follows the subject, there is more information provided between them. This information, in most cases, is not essential and could be left out entirely without affecting the meaning of the sentence. However, this style allows you to expand on your simple sentences, thus creating longer, more fact-filled sentences, and adding versatility and variety to your writing style.

■ **Examples:** (subjects are underlined once; verbs, twice)

a) The <u>boy</u> who lives next door <u>is</u> my best friend.

The boy is my friend would be the simple, natural format of the sentence. By adding *who lives next door*, you are describing the bare subject before moving on to the verb.

b) Rudyard Kipling, a famous British poet, wrote the poem "If."

A famous British poet further explains or elaborates on the subject, *Rudyard Kipling*, so that the reader knows a little bit more about him. Such phrases or clauses are known as **appositives** or **words in apposition**.

c) Joyce Lauron, who is my teacher, has just won an Olympic gold medal.

Again, if the reader had heard of Joyce Lauron, and knew the author of this sentence, the split format would give him or her a little more information about both the subject and the author. It also makes the sentence a little more interesting.

d) The party, incidentally, will begin at 8:00 P.M. tonight.

e) You, of course, will accompany me to Vancouver.

By now you should have several ways of gaining both variety and flexibility in sentence structure. You should be able to write sentences without always beginning them with a subject/verb word order.

EXERCISE 9.4.1

In a sentence, explain the format used (natural, inverted, or split) in each of the following sentences:

1. What are you doing?

_____

2. You are late for class.

_____

3. *Gone with the Wind* is a movie classic.

_____

4. Are you learning much this semester?

_____

5. Dr. Jones, who is a brilliant surgeon, is my uncle.

_____

9.5   COMPOUND SUBJECTS AND COMPOUND PREDICATES

COMPOUND SUBJECTS

"Compound" means "having more than one part." It follows, therefore, that a **compound subject** contains more than one subject—usually two or more nouns. (see Module 8 for more discussion on this topic.) Here is an example:

Pliers, a screwdriver, and a wrench are in her tool kit.

There is no single subject in this sentence. The sentence is about three things: the pliers, the screwdriver, and the wrench. Since there is more than one subject, the subject is said to be compound.

Grouping words together in this fashion will cut down on the number of words used and will thus create a tighter writing style.

EXERCISE 9.5.1

In the following sentences, underline the compound subjects once. Explain your answers in a sentence.

1. The girls, but not the boys, were always on time.

   _____

   _____

2. In the parade were both soldiers and pilots.

   _____

   _____

3. There will always be wars and rumours of wars.

   _____

   _____

4. Britons and Russians fought on the same side in World War II.

   _____

   _____

5. After the game, players and coaches shook hands.

   _____

   _____

COMPOUND PREDICATES (VERBS)

Just as you can decrease the number of words used by compounding subjects, you can do the same by compounding verbs. For example:

Last Monday, Colette washed and ironed all her bed linen.

There are two verbs in this sentence. These are the actions *washed* and *ironed*. Since there are more actions than just one, the verb, or predicate, is said to be **compound**.

EXERCISE 9.5.2

In the following sentences, underline the compound predicates twice. Explain your answers in a sentence.

1. He showered and then ate a steak and kidney pie.

_____

_____

2. After drawing money out of the bank, she wandered through a suburban mall and visited three boutiques.

_____

_____

3. On Wednesday, she went to the library, looked at several magazines, and attended a lecture.

_____

_____

4. In the course of a week, my mother went to the opera, attended a political meeting, gave a party, and saw two plays.

_____

_____

5. For Thursday night dinner, mother cooks roast beef and prepares Yorkshire pudding, baked potatoes, and green peas to go with it.

_____

_____

EXERCISE 9.5.3

Underline the compound bare subjects once and the compound bare predicates twice in the following sentences.

■ **Example:**

The men and women are dancing and clapping to the music.

1. The boys and girls are playing and singing during recess.

2. My mother and I drink lots of water and eat an apple every day.

3. Captive birds and animals long for the open air and thus seek to escape their cages.

4. My favourite TV movies and films give me a happy sense of life and tend to lift my spirits.

5. What do teachers and professors think of museums and feel about art galleries?

9.6   MODIFIERS

To modify means to change the meaning of another word. A **modifier** is a word (or group of words) that describes, adds information, or limits the meaning of another word. Modifiers are usually one of two kinds:

1. adjectives, which modify nouns or pronouns; and

2. adverbs, which modify verbs, adjectives, or other adverbs.

(See Module 4 for a full discussion of adverbs and adjectives.)

COMMON ERROR—MISPLACED MODIFIERS

Modifiers must be placed directly before the word they modify; if this is not done, the meaning can be seriously affected. For instance, note the following examples and their respective meanings when using the modifying word "only":

Only he told Ellen what to do.	(Nobody else told her.)
He told only Ellen what to do.	(He did not tell anybody else.)
He told Ellen only what he knew.	(He did not tell anything else.)
He told Ellen what only he knew.	(Nobody else knew it.)

A modifier can also be a group of words, for example:

(With obvious strength), (the tall and rather heavy) weightlifter lunged (at the burglar).

Note that *with obvious strength* and *at the burglar* are groups of words that modify the verb *lunged*, and are therefore **adverbial modifiers**. On the other hand, *the tall and rather heavy* modifies the noun *weightlifter*, and is therefore an **adjectival modifier**. (See Module 4, "Adjectives and Adverbs," for further clarification.)

Curious, sometimes funny, things happen if modifiers are placed too far away from the words they are supposed to modify. Consider the following example:

I am not amused at dinner parties where the hostess serves her guests on paper napkins rather than on china plates.

In this sentence, the phrase *on paper napkins rather than on china plates* is modifying the noun *guests*, which means that the guests are being served up on paper napkins! (See Module 7 for a discussion of phrases.)

EXERCISE 9.6.1

Put parentheses ( ) around the misplaced modifiers in the following sentences and square brackets [ ] around the word or words they logically modify.

1. Mrs. Salazar writes to her niece, who lives in Maine, almost every day.

2. She only studied misplaced modifiers last night.

3. In our organization is a young group of men and women.

4. He gave him an amicable pat as he left the pool on his back.

5. A woman was ambling along the road wearing too much makeup.

9.7   SENTENCE FRAGMENTS

Every sentence must have a subject and a verb, and must express a complete thought. A word group that lacks either a subject or a verb, and does not express a complete thought, is a **fragment**.

Reread your writing to make certain that you have not written a fragment. Make sure that every sentence you write has both a subject and a verb *and* expresses a complete thought. The most common types of fragments are dependent word fragments; *-ing*, and *to* fragments; and added-detail fragments.

DEPENDENT WORD FRAGMENTS

A list of common dependent words that cause fragments, especially when they begin a group of words, are as follows:

after	if, even if	when, whenever
although, though	in order that	where, wherever
as	since	whether, which, whichever
because	that, so that	while
before	unless	who, whose
even though	until	
how	what, whatever	

Whenever you start a sentence using one of these words, you must be careful that a fragment does not result. Be sure that your group of words contains both a subject and a verb and that the main idea of the sentence is clear and complete.

To correct the fragment, follow through and complete the thought:

> After I came inside. (fragment)

> After I came inside, it stopped raining.

Use a comma after an introductory subordinate clause.

EXERCISE 9.7.1

Turn each of the dependent word groups into a sentence by adding a complete thought.

■ **Example:**

Although I finished working on Friday

Although I finished working on Friday, my official vacation will begin only on Monday.

1. Because it was snowing

   _____

2. Before I left the house

   _____

3. When I had an accident on the highway

   _____

4. The department store to which I went

   _____

5. The instructor who gave me the highest mark

   _____

EXERCISE 9.7.2

Correct each fragment by combining it with the sentence that comes before or after—whichever sounds more natural. Answers will vary.

1. Although the heat was on. I still felt cold in the room. I wondered if I had a fever.

   _____

   _____

2. When John got into his car this morning. He discovered that he had left the windows open. The seats and rug were full of snow. Since it snowed overnight.

   _____

   _____

3. Tom skimmed out the soggy leaves. They were at the bottom of the pool. He was about to vacuum next. When two bullfrogs jumped out at him. He dropped the vacuum and ran into the house.

4. After cutting fish at the restaurant all day. Nadia smelled like a fish factory. She could not wait to take a hot, perfumed bath.

5. Because he had drunk too much. He had to have a friend drive him home. His head, which began to pound. That was ready to explode.

-ING AND *TO* FRAGMENTS

When a word ending in *-ing* appears at the beginning of a word group, a fragment may result.

Incorrect: I spent all day cleaning. Trying to get my house ready in time for my guests.

Correct: I spent all day cleaning, trying to get my house ready in time for my guests.

Can you see the difference between these two examples? Look for the bare subject and bare predicate. Remember that verbs are not the same thing as verbals, and that to be a complete sentence and not just a fragment, a clause or sentence must contain a subject and a main verb. When an infinitive, participle, or gerund appears at or near the beginning of a word group, a fragment may result.

Incorrect: 1. To eat his favourite food. Ron went to an Italian restaurant.

2. Applying for a job at the factory. Krystyna made her application early.

3. On hearing that she had won the lottery. Tasha immediately phoned her husband to tell him the good news.

Correct: 1. To eat his favourite food, Ron went to an Italian restaurant.

2. Applying for a job at the factory, Salama made her application early.

3. On hearing that she had won the lottery, Tasha immediately phoned her husband to tell him the good news.

EXERCISE 9.7.3

Underline the *-ing* or *to* fragment in each selection. Then rewrite each selection correctly.

1. Glistening with dew. The immense web hung between the branches of the maple tree. The spider waited patiently for a fly.

_____

_____

2. Shari picked through the box of cookies. Removing the ones she did not like. She saved the balance for her family.

_____

_____

3. Andrew went quickly to the bank. To deposit his paycheque. Otherwise, he would have no money to cover the cheques he wrote.

_____

_____

4. My feet suddenly sank into the cement I was walking on. Because the workers had just poured it and had not had time to put up a sign saying "Wet cement."

_____

_____

5. Martha is pleased with her newly painted house. Claiming that her husband did a good job.

_____

_____

ADDED-DETAIL FRAGMENTS

Added-detail fragments often begin with:

also	except	including
especially	for example	such as

Incorrect: Yuri has trouble accepting criticism. Except from Betty. She is his wife.

Correct: Yuri has trouble accepting criticism, except from his wife, Betty.

Except from Betty is a prepositional phrase that has neither a subject nor a predicate; therefore, this is a sentence fragment.

Incorrect: My house has one drawback. For example, no air conditioning in the summer.

Correct: My house has one drawback: no air conditioning in the summer.

For example, no air conditioning in the summer contains a subject but has no predicate. A sentence missing either of these is a fragment.

EXERCISE 9.7.4

Rewrite the following sentences, eliminating all fragments. Answers may vary.

1. My dog is always into mischief. Such as stealing, and chewing shoes.

_____

_____

2. Alex's job in the customer complaint department is difficult. Complaints about missing parts, rude salespeople, damaged goods. Go on all day.

_____

_____

3. My mother is still street-proofing me. For example, not talking to strangers. But I sometimes ignore her.

_____

_____

4. My father said to get a good education. Including such jobs as doctor, lawyer, and teacher. I now know that he was right.

_____

_____

EXERCISE 9.7.5

Correct the following missing-subject fragments. Rewrite the selections correctly in the spaces provided.

1. Dulce went to the cupboard to get some sugar for the fruit. And discovered nothing left in the container.

_____

_____

2. I put my money into the photocopier and loaded the papers. Then saw the "Out of Order" sign taped to the cover.

_____

_____

3. Our next-door neighbours suddenly moved this weekend. But did not tell us where they were going. We all wondered what had happened.

_____

_____

4. Mary's daughter could not accept her mother's marrying again. Also was constantly criticizing her choice of husband.

_____

_____

5. Nick stared at the first question on the exam. And decided that he should have studied harder.

_____

_____

9.8   COMMONLY CONFUSED WORDS

Using the wrong word can also change the meaning and affect the clarity of a sentence. Errors in word choice are usually made because two words have similar meanings, or the words sound or look alike. Below is a list of some of the most commonly confused words:

1. *A* is an article used before a word that begins with a consonant sound.
   e.g., a girl, a city, a mountain

   An is an article used before a word that begins with a vowel sound.
   e.g., an octopus, an animal, an hour (the word *hour* starts with a vowel sound, but the first letter is a consonant)

2. *Accept* is a verb meaning "to receive."
   e.g., He accepted the new job.

   Except is a preposition meaning "not included."
   e.g., All my friends except David came to the party.

3. *Affect* is a verb meaning "to influence."
   e.g., The decision will affect her future.

   Effect is generally a noun meaning "result." It can be used as a verb when it means "to cause."
   e.g., The effect of the storm was devastating.

4. *Already* means "by this time" or "before a specified time."
   e.g., She was already late for work.

   All ready means "being prepared."
   e.g., They were all ready to leave on their holiday.

5. *Among* is used when discussing three or more things.
   e.g., The offer divides the profit among the shareholders.

   Between is used when discussing two things.
   e.g., She had to decide between the red dress and the black suit.

6. *Are* is a linking verb.
   e.g., They are going to leave.

   Our is a possessive pronoun that is used as an adjective.
   e.g., It is our house.

7. *Bought* means "purchased."
   e.g., Chris bought a new car.

   Brought means "caused to come."
   e.g., They brought their dog with them.

8. *Brake* can be used as a noun or verb and refers to a device that makes things stop.
   e.g., The brakes on my car need to be replaced. (noun)
       I braked to avoid hitting the raccoon. (verb)

Break as a noun refers to "an interruption."
e.g., We took a break before we reached the summit.

As a verb *break* means "to separate from something" or "to crack or shatter."
e.g., I had to break the window to get into the house.

9. *In* means "located within something."
   e.g., The Eaton Centre is in Toronto.

   Into means "toward the inside."
   e.g., I walked into the store.

10. *Its* is the possessive form of the pronoun *it*.
    e.g., She liked its colour.

    It's is a contraction meaning *it is*.
    e.g., It's going to be a warm day.

11. *Passed* is the past tense form of the verb *pass*. It means *went by*.
    e.g., They passed the road where they were supposed to turn.

    Past refers to something that has ended or gone by.
    e.g., The accident was part of his past.

12. *Than* is a conjunction used to imply a comparison.
    e.g., The coffee was hotter than the soup.

    Then means "next" or "at that time."
    e.g., He went to the store and then to the gym.

13. *Their* is the possessive form of the pronoun *they*.
    e.g., It is their property.

    There refers to a location, "in that place."
    e.g., There are the new houses.

    They're is a contraction for "they are."
    e.g., They're walking to work.

14. *To* is a preposition meaning "towards."
    e.g., Mike went to Ottawa on the weekend.

    Too means "more than enough" or "also."
    e.g., It was too cold to go outside.
       I went to Ottawa too.

    Two refers to the number.
    e.g., I have two cats.

15. *Were* is a past tense linking verb.
    e.g., They were left outside overnight.

    We're is a contraction for "we are."
    e.g., We're good friends.

Where refers to a place.
e.g., That is where I grew up.

16. *Your* is the possessive form of the pronoun *you*.
e.g., It is your choice.

You're is the contraction form of *you are*.
e.g., I hear you're leaving tomorrow.

EXERCISE 9.8.1

Underline the correct word in parentheses, and in a sentence explain your decision.

1. IBM is (an, a) international company.

_____

_____

2. (There, They're, Their) hoping to go to the Caribana parade.

_____

_____

3. She got (too, to, two) tickets for the theatre.

_____

_____

4. The money will be divided (between, among) the three winners.

_____

_____

5. I like all the seasons, (accept, except) winter.

_____

_____

6. The hockey players (we're, were, where) exhausted after the long road trip.

_____

_____

ANSWER KEY

EXERCISE 9.1.1

1. <u>Kumar</u> <u>went</u> to the ballet twice last week.
3. <u>(You)</u> <u>Go</u> to the corner store for some Lifesavers.
5. <u>(You)</u> <u>Sit</u> up straight in your seat, Darin.

EXERCISE 9.1.2

1. <u>Occasionally</u>, <u>Dr. Ramjeet's class</u> <u>is taken out into the country to study nature</u>.
3. <u>Do</u> <u>you</u> <u>speak Greek, or any other language besides English</u>?
5. <u>Do</u> <u>you</u> <u>ever wonder what</u> <u>it</u> <u>would be like to live on the moon</u>?

EXERCISE 9.2.1

1. interrogative
3. assertive
5. assertive

EXERCISE 9.3.1

1. complex
3. complex
5. compound-complex

EXERCISE 9.4.1

1. inverted
3. natural
5. split

EXERCISE 9.5.1

1. girls, boys
3. wars, rumours
5. players, coaches

EXERCISE 9.5.2

1. showered, ate
3. went, looked, attended
5. cooks, prepares

EXERCISE 9.5.3

1. The <u>boys and girls</u> <u>are playing and singing</u> during recess.
3. Captive <u>birds and animals</u> <u>long</u> for the open air and thus seek to escape their cages.
5. What do <u>teachers and professors</u> <u>think</u> of museums <u>and feel</u> about art galleries?

EXERCISE 9.6.1

1. Mrs. Salazar [writes] to her niece, who lives in Maine, (almost every day).
3. (In our organization) is a (young) group of [men and women].
5. A [woman] was ambling along the road (wearing too much makeup).

EXERCISE 9.7.1–9.7.5

Answers will vary.

EXERCISE 9.8.1

1. an
3. two
5. except

MODULE 10

PUNCTUATION AND CAPITALIZATION

Learning Outcome Statement

By successfully completing a series of module exercises, you will demonstrate your ability to punctuate and to use capital letters correctly.

PUNCTUATION AND CAPITALIZATION

Let us pretend there was no such thing as punctuation we would never be able to tell when a sentence began or ended nor would we be able to express in writing all of the subtle shades of meaning in spoken english what do you think the world would be like it is hard to imagine

Now, let's try that again:

Let us pretend there was no such thing as punctuation! We would never be able to tell when a sentence began or ended; nor would we be able to express in writing all of the subtle shades of meaning in spoken English. What do you think the world would be like? It is hard to imagine.

Written English is a substitute for spoken English. When we are face to face with our audience, we can use eye contact and speech emphasis to enhance and clarify the meaning of what we are trying to say. For instance, few people talk without using their hands for emphasis, and no one speaks in a complete monotone.

In written communication, we do not have tools like hands, facial expressions, or spoken tone to help us communicate. Instead, we must use punctuation to help our message. We are also less sure of who our audience may be. Once something is written down, we may have very little control over who receives our communication.

To have our writing make sense and be instantly clear, we must make use of a grammatical "shorthand" consisting of punctuation marks and capital letters. This module will cover the more common uses of capitalization and punctuation. It is not intended to be complete and exhaustive.

Punctuation and capitalization were invented to make the meaning of your writing instantly clear. Familiarize yourself, therefore, with the guidelines of their usage. The punctuation you use will depend on your choice of words and your sentence structure.

10.1   CAPITALIZATION

The various uses of capitalization are outlined below.

FIRST WORD OF A SENTENCE

When starting a sentence of any kind (an assertion, a question, a command, or an exclamation), it is important to indicate to your reader that a new thought is beginning. This is done by capitalizing the first letter of the first word of the sentence.

■ **Examples:**

They went to a movie.	(assertion)
What are you doing?	(question)
Sit down.	(command)
What a beautiful day!	(exclamation)

DIRECT QUOTATIONS

Sentences enclosed within quotation marks are capitalized as they would be without quotation marks.

■ **Examples:**

With quotation marks:	"**We** are very tired," the children complained, "and we want to go home."
Without quotation marks:	**We** are very tired, and we want to go home.

PROPER NOUNS (NAMES OF PERSONS, PLACES, OR THINGS)

The key to understanding proper nouns is their specificity; for example, if we discuss the fact that Canada has ten provinces, we need not capitalize the word "province" because we are not discussing a specific province. However, if we wish to talk about Ontario, we use a capital letter to highlight the fact that we are discussing a specific province, the province of Ontario. Other uses of capital letters for proper nouns are shown in the following examples:

- names of people (Margaret, Muhammad)

- a title used before a name (Doctor Domville, Professor Grant, Prime Minister Chrétien)

- the personal pronoun *I*

- names of months, days of the week, and holidays (October, Tuesday, Christmas)

- names of ethnic groups and languages (Jewish, French)

- names of specific historical events and documents (World War II, War of 1812, Magna Carta)

- words that refer to a supreme being (God, Krishna), religious denominations (Buddhist, Hindu), and sacred books (Koran, Bible, Torah)

TITLES (CAPITALIZE FIRST, LAST, AND IMPORTANT WORDS)

The title may be of a play, a book, a song or poem, movies, television programs, compact discs, and tapes. Do not capitalize short prepositions (*to, for, at*), short coordinating conjunctions (*and, or, but, for*), or articles (*a, an, the*) unless they appear as the first or last word of the title.

Note which words are capitalized in the following examples:

a)	*King Arthur and the Knights of the Round Table*	(literary work)
b)	*In Search of...*	(television show)
c)	*Schindler's List*	(movie and book)

OTHER RULES OF CAPITALIZATION

1. Do not capitalize the names of the seasons (spring, summer, autumn, winter), or directions (north, etc.), unless referring to seasons used as characters (see (b) below), or specific geographical areas (see (d) below).

> a) It was going to be a chilly autumn.
>
> b) It seemed as if Autumn were painting the trees.
>
> c) We headed south on the highway.
>
> d) We spent a week in the Deep South of the United States.

2. Do not capitalize the names of games or sports unless the name is a trademark.

> After dinner, we played Trivial Pursuit, Monopoly, checkers, bridge, and dominoes.

EXERCISE 10.1.1

Rewrite the following sentences, making corrections in capitalization as required.

1. whenever i go to toronto, i always like to walk down yonge street past the eaton centre.

_____

_____

2. if dr. martin prescribes an antibiotic, you should take it before you fly to aruba.

_____

_____

3. the great wall of china is one of the seven wonders of the world.

_____

_____

4. i went shopping with my sister charity.

_____

_____

5. i went shopping with sister charity.

_____

_____

10.2 PUNCTUATION

Punctuation operates like road signs in your sentences. It guides the reader through a potential maze of words to your specific meaning.

THE PERIOD (.)

In our writing, we must give a sign to the reader that a thought or idea is complete. In speech this would be given by a pause, or by voice tone or inflection. In writing we must use something that can be seen by the eye: a **period**, or **full stop**.

Use a period to end a statement or command.

■ **Examples:**

> Close the door, please.
>
> I was so busy that I didn't have time to call.

Use a period after most abbreviations.

■ **Examples:**

> Dr. Wu,
>
> Prof. Grant,
>
> P.M. Chrétien
>
> Mrs. Ngo (or Ms. Ngo)

> *NOTES:* Abbreviations that are extremely common will often not make use of a period; for example, IBM, NATO, TV, UN.
>
> It is not appropriate to use abbreviations in any type of formal letter or paper, with the exception of certain titles (Mr., Mrs., Ms., Dr.) and certain Latin short forms: *etc.* for *et cetera*, *i.e.* for *id est* (*that is*), or *e.g.* for *for example*, among others. In written English most of these should be used in their long form, or avoided completely.

THE QUESTION MARK (?)

Not all sentences end with a period. If your sentence is interrogative, place **a question mark** (**?**) at the end of the question. In speech, the vocal inflection (a rise in pitch at the end of the question) would reveal the question, and thus differentiate it from a statement.

> There are none left?   (requests information)
>
> There are none left.   (provides information)

When a question is part of a statement, it is called *an indirect question*, and no question mark is needed:

> Is she hungry?   (direct question)
>
> He wondered if she was hungry.   (indirect question)

THE EXCLAMATION MARK (!)

When writers wish to express strong emotion or excitement, or to emphasize a sentence, they use an **exclamation mark** (!) at the end of the sentence.

■ **Examples:**

There is a car behind you.   (providing information)

There is a car behind you!   (warning, conveying emotion)

Read the following sentences and imagine the difference with and without exclamation marks.

He had enough

Go home

Do not cross the road

I do not want any

EXERCISE 10.2.1

Rewrite the following sentences, placing the correct punctuation mark(s) at the appropriate point in the following sentences.

1. Why does he always make a mistake

_____

_____

2. Marikka was not sure if she believed the story

_____

_____

3. I cannot believe she told me such a bold-faced lie

_____

_____

4. May we not speed up a little

_____

_____

5. "Where was the dog" he asked

_____

THE COLON (:)

The main function of the colon is to "announce" something to come. It indicates that the list, quotation, or examples that follow are directly related to the statement just written. The colon often replaces the words "that is to say" or "for example."

■ **Examples:**

a) The hikers saw only two options for crossing the river: (that is to say) swim across or take the long route to the bridge.

b) These are people you will encounter at work: (that is to say) your supervisors, your co-workers, and possibly your staff.

c) He referred to that old adage: (that is to say) "There's no use crying over spilled milk."

d) God is not mocked: (that is to say) whatsoever ye sow, that shall ye also reap.

Another use of the colon is to separate the figures that denote hours, minutes, and seconds; volumes and pages of magazines or other publications; and chapters and verses of the Bible or other religious books.

■ **Examples:**

a) His plane arrived at precisely 11:22:30 p.m.

b) The article appeared in Volume 14:256.

c) The pastor referred to John 1:23 in the New Testament.

EXERCISE 10.2.2

Rewrite the following sentences, putting in colons wherever they are needed. Also, add capitalization and any other punctuation you have learned so far.

1. the following items are needed sugar, milk, and bread

_____

_____

2. dear sir this is my last will and testament

_____

_____

3. how could you do that to me leave me alone at night

_____

_____

4. what you say is true we must prepare for winter

_____

_____

5. the minister read from exodus 2 20 at 11 00 a m on sunday

_____

_____

THE SEMICOLON (;)

The colon and the semicolon have similar main uses. Do not, however, confuse these two punctuation marks. Their uses are quite separate and different.

There are three main uses for the semicolon:

1. To replace a missing coordinate conjunction between two principal clauses.

■ **Examples:**

   a) The car was old; it needed repairs.

The semicolon replaces the missing coordinate conjunction *and* between the two principal clauses: *The car was old* and *it needed repairs.*

   b) I cannot attend the meeting; my brother will go instead.

The semicolon replaces the missing coordinate conjunction *but* between the two principal clauses: *I cannot attend the meeting* and *my brother will go instead.*

2. To replace a missing coordinate conjunction immediately before a transitional word or word group (also known as an adverbial connective). Like (1) above, these transitional words must sit directly between the two main clauses. Some of these transitional words and word groups are: *as a result, consequently, hence, however, in addition, moreover, therefore,* and *thus.* Such transitional words are preceded by a semicolon and followed by a comma. (See "The Comma" in the following section.)

■ **Examples:**

   a) The car was old; **thus**, it needed repairs.

The semicolon replaces *and* between the two principal clauses.

   b) I cannot go; **however**, my brother will be there.

The semicolon replaces *but* between the two principal clauses.

   c) He tried hard; **moreover**, he won the pole vault.

Once again, the semicolon replaces *and* between the two main clauses.

3. Groups of words about related things are separated by semicolons, especially if any of the word groups already contains commas. This should help to avoid confusion for the reader.

■ **Examples:**

a) Orders came in on January 4, 1994; June 6, 1994; November 12, 1994; and March 30, 1995.

b) A young puppy requires many things: food and water; a warm place to sleep; vaccination papers and a licence; something to play with, such as a ball, a bone, or a squeaky toy; and most of all, lots of love.

c) You will find references to politics in paragraph 2, page 39; paragraph 6, page 51; and paragraph 3, page 63.

Note how much easier it is to read (and hence to understand) these sentences when the major divisions end with semicolons.

EXERCISE 10.2.3

Insert semicolons and colons where needed in the following sentences.

1. I can go my brother cannot.

2. She sent letters on the following dates March 29, 1989 April 16, 1990 September 14, 1991 and October 21, 1992.

3. He wandered around the huge supermarket and purchased the following different kinds of items pens, pencils, and scratch pads hardware tools, insulation, and paint and videotapes, audiotapes, and CD's.

4. She saw him he did not see her.

5. I have done wrong consequently I shall have to pay for my acts.

THE COMMA (,)

The period, question mark, exclamation mark, semicolon, and colon denote major pauses in your written work. The **comma** is used for minor pauses. It has several uses, each of which will be studied in turn.

Words, Phrases, and Clauses in a Series

Words, phrases, and clauses in a series are separated by commas, with the final comma coming just before the coordinate conjunction *and*.

■ **Examples:**

a) She bought peanuts, popcorn, and chewing gum. (words in a series)

b) In this game of hide-and-seek, in the basement, behind the garage, and on the roof are off-limits. (prepositional phrases in a series)

c) Running errands, doing dishes, and washing the dirty laundry are all part of a day's work for her. (gerund phrases in a series)

d) He went to work, tutored his son, and helped his wife every day. (coordinate clauses in a series)

e) He said that he drank two cups of coffee every morning, that he ate very little food at noon, and that he always enjoyed a big meal at dinner time. (subordinate clauses in a series)

Note that in all of the above examples each unit is followed by a comma. Note also that in every example there is a comma before *and*.

Commas After Introductory Word Groups

A comma follows an introductory subordinate clause or an introductory verbal phrase. A comma does not usually follow an introductory prepositional phrase unless there are two or more such phrases strung together.

■ **Examples:**

a) Before you start doing your homework, please wash the dishes. (comma after an introductory subordinate clause)

b) By working late, you are setting a good example for other staff members. (comma after introductory gerund phrase)

c) Having arrived at the airport early, she had time for a light snack. (comma after an introductory participial phrase)

d) To be absolutely accurate, she always checked her work twice. (comma after an introductory infinitive phrase)

e) During the day he became ill. (no punctuation necessary after a single introductory prepositional phrase)

f) In the heat of the night, he had a bad dream. (comma after two joined introductory prepositional phrases)

> *NOTE:* If the above subordinate clauses, verbal phrases, and linked prepositional phrases had come at the end of the sentence, rather than at the beginning, there would be no punctuation in any of the examples, other than the period at the end.

Interrupted Thought

Words, phrases, and clauses that interrupt the smooth flow of thought are set off by commas.

■ **Examples:**

a) We would like you to speak tonight or, if you prefer, tomorrow night.

b) It is wise, is it not, to think before speaking.

c) Thanh Chung, rather than Bill Harris, won the scholarship.

Words, phrases, and clauses added as an afterthought at the end of a sentence are preceded by a comma.

■ **Examples:**

a) Take a look at that table, please.

b) I would like you to clean the sink, if you do not mind.

c) You have not closed the store yet, have you?

When we studied the uses of the colon, you learned that transitional words sitting between two principal clauses were preceded by a semicolon and followed by a comma. If such words are placed within a clause, they are set off by commas.

■ **Examples:**

a) I cannot, however, do what you ask. (interjection within a principal clause)

b) If, moreover, what you say is true, you have no worries about losing your job. (interjection within a subordinate clause)

c) I must say, nonetheless, that his work is unacceptable.

d) It is, of course, your right to complain.

e) I cannot, therefore, grant your request.

Principal Clauses Joined by Conjunctions

When two or more principal clauses are joined by coordinate conjunctions, and the subjects of those clauses are different, a comma will precede the conjunction.

■ **Examples:**

a) I am leaving, but my sister is staying.

b) I wrote to him, and Bill spoke to her.

c) She does not care, nor does he.

d) I wrote to him but I spoke to her.

NOTE: If the subjects of the two clauses are the same, especially if the clauses are short, no punctuation is necessary. See (d) in the examples above.

Separating Adjectives

A comma is used to separate two adjectives that modify the same noun.

■ **Examples:**

a) The quiet, meandering brook made me think of spring.

b) For his birthday I bought him an expensive, stylish suit and black, shiny shoes.

c) The wealthy, wandering pop star played in Hamilton last night.

Nonrestrictive Clauses

Nonrestrictive adjectival clauses are set off by commas.

■ **Examples:**

a) Steve Lui, who happens to be my assistant, is ill at the moment.

b) The reporter interviewed Kimo Ng, who was on duty that night, and then phoned in his column to the city desk.

    c) *The Toronto Star*, which is Canada's largest newspaper, has many employees.

Appositives

Words in apposition (words placed beside other words to amplify their meaning by presenting additional information) are set off by commas.

■ **Examples:**

    a) Dr. Chung, a brilliant acupuncturist, told me a story about his youth in China.

    b) She visited McCaulay Worthington, a famous stage actor, at his home in New York.

    c) That book, *Gone with the Wind*, has sold millions of copies since it was first published in 1937.

Words of Direct Address

Words that directly address people are set off by commas.

■ **Examples:**

    a) Go to the store, Sally, and buy some strawberries.

    b) Look at the board, children, and read aloud what is written there.

    c) I cannot understand, mother, why you would say that.

In the above examples *Sally*, *children*, and *mother* are all directly addressed by name.

Dates

Commas are used to separate days, months, and years in dates.

■ **Examples:**

    a) Pamela will be home from university for spring break on Friday, March 10, 1995.

    b) At the top of the letter the date read: January 27, 1780.

    c) He visited us on Saturday, December 31, 1994, and again on Monday, January 2, 1995.

Direct Speech in Quotation Marks

Commas are used before quotation marks and after the interjected words in interrupted speech.

■ **Examples:**

    a) "I cannot go to the party," she wept, "because my dearest friend has been in a tragic accident."

    b) "What do you think," he muttered, "would be the result of such a lie?"

c) "Get out of my sight," she shouted, "and never come back!"

> *NOTE:* Although there are several other uses of the comma, the rules described earlier should be all you need for the time being. Should you have any problems, consult your instructor.

EXERCISE 10.2.4

Rewrite and punctuate the following sentences, paying special attention to commas.

1. at the market they bought tomatoes cucumbers and celery

_____

2. after the war was over were many people out of work

_____

3. my nephew is sick but my niece his sister is in excellent health

_____

4. because he was ill he did not go to work on thursday march 9 or on friday march 10

_____

5. the class boys and girls is now dismissed for recess

_____

EXERCISE 10.2.5

Rewrite the following sentences, placing colons, semicolons, and commas in the correct places.

1. I cannot be with you I have a previous appointment.

_____

2. Only one thing was evident her guilt.

_____

_____

3. Three desirable qualities in a dog are the following intelligence loyalty and friendliness.

_____

_____

4. The woman was very nasty she must be bitter or crazy.

_____

_____

5. He quoted Hamlet's famous line "To be or not to be."

_____

_____

THE APOSTROPHE (')

The **apostrophe** has two main uses: to indicate possession or ownership and to show plurals of numbers, letters, and words referred to as words.

Possession or Ownership

Use an apostrophe to indicate possession or ownership. For example, "Joan's book" means "the book owned by Joan." "Carlos's dog" means "the dog owned by Carlos." The apostrophized word is said to be in the possessive case. Apostrophes are used only with nouns. (For further information on cases of nouns, see Module 1.)

Once you have determined whether a noun is singular or plural, then you can determine the form of its possessive case.

■ **Examples:**

Singular Noun	Possessive Case	Plural Noun	Possessive Case
woman	woman's	women	women's
class	class's	classes	classes'
dog	dog's	dogs	dogs'
lens	lens's	lenses	lenses'

A common error is to confuse *its* (possessive adjective) and *it's*. The latter always means *it is* since the apostrophe replaces the *i*. The possessive form of the pronoun is never written with an apostrophe. Remember also that the contraction *it's* should never be used in formal written style.

When working with the concept of possession or ownership, keep in mind the practical reality of whether or not a thing can be owned by more than one person.

■ **Examples:**

Wrong: The duchesses' gown was beautiful.

Right: The duchess's gown was beautiful. (one gown, one duchess)

The duchesses' gowns were beautiful. (more than one gown, more than one duchess)

The thief's car broke down during the getaway. (one thief, one car)

The thieves' car broke down during the getaway. (more than one thief, only one car)

When dealing with possession by more than one person, use the apostrophe carefully:

John and Mary's car   Both share one car.

John and Mary's cars   Both share ownership of more than one car.

John's and Mary's cars   Both own their own cars separately.

Numbers, Letters, and Words Referred to as Words

Use an apostrophe to indicate plurals of numbers, letters, and words referred to as words.

■ **Examples:**

a) He has thoroughly learned his ABC's.

b) There are three 5's in that equation.

c) There are two the's in that sentence.

EXERCISE 10.2.6

Give the possessive plurals of the following words; then use each in a sentence.

1. teacher

_____

_____

2. class

_____

_____

3. mother-in-law

_____

_____

4. child

_____

_____

5. crisis

_____

_____

PARENTHESES ( )

Parentheses are used before and after a word, phrase, or sentence that interrupts a thought pattern either to explain something further or to modify a given thought.

■ **Examples:**

a) The beautiful dark-haired man (whom I had never met before) came over and started talking to me.

b) Maria wrote to tell me that she, her husband, and her two sons (or were they daughters?) had toured Europe on bicycles.

c) Even though she was tired (she had worked hard all day), she went dancing Friday night.

As you can see, the information provided in parentheses is not essential to the sentence, but instead simply adds to the total mental picture.

Do not overuse parentheses, especially where commas are a better substitute. More-over, remember that periods and commas that are part of the information enclosed in parentheses should remain outside of the parentheses (see example (c) above).

EXERCISE 10.2.7

Insert parentheses where needed in the following sentences:

1. The new outfit actually a dress did not fit her well.

2. Jasmine who must be her daughter was sent to her room by the angry woman.

3. He really appeared scared or so it seemed to me of his father when he had to confront him.

4. Tell me three actually four ways of making this project work.

5. Pay close attention to the exercise it is very important on page 29.

THE DASH (—) AND THE HYPHEN (-)

These are two different punctuation marks and they should not be confused. The **dash** (—) serves a similar function as parentheses ( ). It is an informal mark of punctuation that should be used sparingly to add emphasis or clarity. There are a few specific uses of the dash:

1. Use a dash to indicate a sudden break in your thoughts.

   Let me give you a full description—but perhaps you will not be interested.

2. A dash can introduce a word or group of words that you wish to emphasize.

   If you will not take an airplane or a train to Vancouver, there is only one other alternative—travel by car.

3. Dashes can be used in pairs to set off abrupt, parenthetical ideas.

   I was happy—delighted I should say—with the way you wrote your essay.

In each of these instances, the use of the dash adds an element of surprise and interest.

NOTE: Do not use the dash when the words *to* or *between* could have been used, such as in describing dates.

   May 21 through August 1 (*not* May 21—August 1)

There are two main uses for the hyphen (-).

1. A hyphen splits a word at the end of a syllable when there is not enough space on the written line to accommodate the whole word.

■ **Examples:**

   a) I tried to fit in the entire word, but knew it was impossible.

   b) The constant drops of rain on the roof were monotonous.

You should either break a syllable between two consonants or start a syllable with a consonant. Every syllable must contain a vowel (see the above examples). When in doubt, consult a dictionary that shows word breaks.

2. A hyphen is also part of the spelling of certain words.

■ **Examples:**

many words beginning with "self":
   self-confidence, self-consideration, self-justification
words containing certain prefixes:
   pro-reform, anti-racist, co-worker
words like:
   compound-complex, mother-in-law, thirty-six
Hyphenating should be avoided as much as possible.

EXERCISE 10.2.8

Insert dashes and hyphens wherever they are required in the following sentences:

1. As you pour the foundation fully and before any of it hardens make sure that you spread the concrete evenly.

2. The woman who helped the child what a kind person acted heroically.

3. She screamed wildly it really was quite terrifying!

4. Treat your co workers as you would like to be treated.

5. A compound complex sentence is usually quite long.

QUOTATION MARKS—DOUBLE (") AND SINGLE (')

Use double quotation marks around the exact words of a speaker. If the speaker quotes someone else within his or her own speech, use single quotation marks around the exact words of the quoted speaker.

■ **Examples:**

a) "Where were you," my mother demanded, "when it was time for supper?"

b) My mother demanded, "Where were you when it was time for supper?"

c) "Where were you when it was time for supper?" demanded my mother.

d) Mother told us, "Mrs. Bacchus said right to my face, 'I dislike you intensely'; I shall never speak to her again."

e) "I shall always admire Shakespeare," our professor remarked one day in class, "because of his saying, 'This above all: to thine own self be true,' and I sincerely believe that if one is not true to one-self, then one will never be true to anyone."

f) "All our teacher ever says is 'don't do this and don't do that,' and I'm sick of it," Nellie complained bitterly.

Double quotation marks also surround titles of short stories, essays, songs, magazine articles, and chapter titles of books. Do not, however, put quotation marks around the title of your own paper, unless you are referring to it in another written work.

NOTE: The titles of complete books should be underlined, not put in quotation marks. For example, The Good Earth, David Copperfield, and Les Misérables.

EXERCISE 10.2.9

Rewrite the following questions, inserting the correct punctuation as required:

1. But why demanded Bob did you not tell the police right away

2. Could you come in later today the doctor's receptionist asked

3. Leave my home immediately said Mrs. Mathers angrily

4. Trying to open the window John gasped it is stuck

5. What we have here said the woman is a kitten that needs love

ANSWER KEY

EXERCISE 10.1.1

1. Whenever I go to Toronto, I always like to walk down Yonge Street past the Eaton Centre.
3. The Great Wall of China is one of the Seven Wonders of the World.
5. I went shopping with Sister Charity.

EXERCISE 10.2.1

1. Why does he always make a mistake?
3. I cannot believe she told me such a bold-faced lie!
5. "Where was the dog?" he asked.

EXERCISE 10.2.2

1. The following items are needed: sugar, milk, and bread.
3. How could you do that to me: leave me alone at night?
5. The minister read from Exodus 2:20 at 11:00 a.m. on Sunday.

EXERCISE 10.2.3

1. I can go; my brother cannot.
3. He wandered around the huge supermarket and purchased the following different kinds of items: pens, pencils, and scratch pads; hardware tools, insulation, and paint; and videotapes, audiotapes, and CD's.
5. I have done wrong; consequently, I shall have to pay for my acts.

EXERCISE 10.2.4

1. At the market they bought tomatoes, cucumbers, and celery.
3. My nephew is sick, but my niece, his sister, is in excellent health.
5. The class, boys and girls, is now dismissed for recess.

EXERCISE 10.2.5

1. I cannot be with you; I have a previous appointment.
3. Three desirable qualities in a dog are the following: intelligence, loyalty, and friendliness.
5. He quoted Hamlet's famous line: "To be or not to be."

EXERCISE 10.2.6

Sentence answers will vary.
1. teachers'
3. mothers-in-law's
5. crises'

EXERCISE 10.2.7

1. The new outfit (actually a dress) did not fit her well.
3. He really appeared scared (or so it seemed to me) of his father when he tried to confront him.
5. Pay close attention to the exercise (it is very important) on page 29.

EXERCISE 10.2.8

1. As you pour the foundation—fully and before any of it hardens—make sure that you spread the concrete evenly.
3. She screamed wildly—it really was quite terrifying!
5. A compound-complex sentence is usually quite long.

EXERCISE 10.2.9

1. "But why," demanded Bob, "did you not tell the police right away?"
3. "Leave my home immediately!" said Mrs. Mathers angrily.
5. "What we have here," said the woman, "is a kitten that needs love."

MODULE 11

PARAGRAPHS

Learning Outcome Statement

By successfully completing a series of writing exercises and assignments, you will be able to write well-constructed paragraphs.

PARAGRAPHS

So far, you have learned about the various types of words and groups of words that make up sentences. You have also learned how to use these elements to add variety to your sentence structure. Now it is time to combine these sentences into paragraphs.

The paragraph is an essential tool for writing skilfully. The basic elements of a paragraph are similar to those found in longer compositions or essays. The writing skills that you will learn in this module will help you with the reports and essays that you will write throughout your school years and throughout your professional life.

This module will teach you to write a complete paragraph. To do this you will:

1. narrow the topic to suit audience and purpose;

2. write a topic sentence;

3. gather and select ideas for the body of the paragraph;

4. organize these ideas; and

5. conclude your paragraph.

11.1 AUDIENCE AND PURPOSE

A **paragraph** is a group of sentences that is related to one idea or topic. The length of the paragraph depends on the idea or topic; however, a paragraph should contain at least three sentences, but more often is five to ten sentences long.

To write a paragraph, you must first pick a *topic*. It is important that you pick a topic that will interest you as well as your potential audience.

To communicate effectively with your reader, consider the person for whom you are writing. Make a reader profile. Ask yourself the following questions and write down your answers as completely as possible in point form:

1. *Who is going to read what I have written?*
   Consider different groups, interests, and expectations. Knowing the answer to this question will help you focus your writing on the specific reader for whom you are writing.

2. *What relationship exists between me and my reader?*
   Am I writing a business letter to my employer, a casual letter to my friend, or a formal essay for my instructor? Knowing the answer to this question will help you set the tone.

3. *What else must I consider about my readers?*
   Are my readers friendly, neutral, biased, hostile, old, young, male, or female? Are they all the same gender or age group? Knowing the answers to these questions will help set limitations on the content to be included in your paragraph.

4. *What do my readers already know about the topic?*
Do they know a little or a lot about my subject? You will also need to determine, based on this information, how much you want to tell your reader. This in turn will help you determine just how much information to include.

5. *What can I do to make my writing as effective as possible?*
What techniques or strategies should I use to communicate in an interesting and informative way? Even if you know who your reader is, consider what your relationship is to that reader, and your reader's characteristics and present knowledge. You must be able to communicate the information in an interesting and effective way.

Once you have a topic in mind, narrow it by determining the *purpose* for writing the paragraph. There are generally eight reasons for writing a paragraph:

1. to describe;

2. to narrate (tell a story);

3. to instruct;

4. to compare or contrast two things;

5. to classify;

6. to define;

7. to analyze or explain; or

8. to argue or persuade.

The purpose of each of the following topic sentences is indicated in parentheses, based on its content.

1. Freewriting is a method used to generate ideas about a specific topic.
    (to define)

2. To assemble this bookshelf, follow these six easy steps.
    (to instruct)

3. Felt-tip pens can be classified as either fine or medium point.
    (to classify)

4. The advantage of independent learning is that it allows students to work at their own paces.
    (to persuade)

5. My diet will improve if I follow Canada's Food Guide.
    (to explain or analyze)

6. My friend, Susan, is the funniest girl I know.
    (to describe)

7. Last night was the worst night of my life.
   (to narrate)

8. Apples and oranges have more in common than people think.
   (to compare or contrast)

It is necessary to have a purpose in mind when writing a paragraph. Without narrowing your topic to fit your purpose, your paragraph will be unorganized and will likely make no sense; moreover, it will be too long and will try to cover too much.

Once you have narrowed the topic of your paragraph, learn how to structure it. A paragraph is made up of three parts:

1. the topic sentence;

2. the body; and

3. the concluding or summarizing sentence.

11.2   THE TOPIC SENTENCE

The **topic sentence** is generally found at the beginning of a paragraph. The purpose of a topic sentence is to tell the reader what the rest of the paragraph will be about. The topic sentence should not go into great detail regarding the content of the paragraph. This is the function of the body of the paragraph.

A good topic sentence should:

1. Tell the reader the main idea of the paragraph.

2. Make a point about the topic.

3. Make a statement, neither too broad nor too narrow, that can be effectively covered in one paragraph.

It is important to make your opening sentence interesting enough to attract the attention of the reader. If readers are not interested in the topic, then they will likely not finish reading the rest of what you have written.

NOTE: Remember to get to the point quickly, and to narrow the point clearly.

■ **Examples:**

a) This paragraph will discuss my cat, Neon. (vague)

This topic sentence does not clearly narrow what the paragraph is to be about.

b) I love my cat, Neon, for many reasons. (too broad or too open)

This topic sentence is too broad to be effectively covered in one paragraph.

c) My cat, Neon, loves to be brushed. (good)

This topic sentence states directly and clearly narrows the main idea of the paragraph. It also makes a statement regarding it. The general topic is "My cat, Neon." The specific, narrowed topic is "loves to be brushed."

The sentences below that are good topic sentences have been indicated by *(Yes)*, and those that are not by *(No)*. Why do you think that these are good or bad topic sentences?

    a) This paragraph is about my school. *(No)*

    b) My sister, Susan, has the largest collection of shoes I have ever seen. *(Yes)*

    c) My goal this year is to try to eat more vegetables. *(Yes)*

    d) The government will be increasing our taxes next year in several ways. *(No)*

    e) This paragraph will discuss opera. *(No)*

> ***NOTE:*** Never start your topic sentence with "This paragraph is about" or "I am going to discuss." These are wasted words. Do not state what you are going to do. Just do it. If you have written a proper topic sentence, your topic should be obvious.

Remember, the topic sentence must be direct, clear, and specific. Look closely at the topic sentences that were good. Notice that they met all the criteria that we discussed above. The other topic sentences did not state a clear and direct topic, nor did they make a statement about the topic. In sentence (d), the topic was far too broad to be effectively covered in one paragraph.

11.3   THE BODY OF THE PARAGRAPH

The purpose of the body of the paragraph is to explain and support the idea presented in the topic sentence. Two good ways to develop ideas for the body of your paragraph are freewriting (unfocused and focused) and brainstorming.

UNFOCUSED FREEWRITING

Unfocused freewriting is simply writing down all your ideas on a page—a sort of "stream of consciousness" off the top of your head. The key to this is not to stop writing while jotting down your ideas. Do not worry about capitalization and punctuation. Once you have written for approximately five minutes, stop and look over what you have put down on paper. You should find one or two (maybe more) ideas on which to build a topic sentence and a paragraph. Underline them as they may well be the basis for focused freewriting (see below). Freewriting is really a preliminary exercise, like playing scales on a musical instrument before you actually play a piece.

FOCUSED FREEWRITING

In **focused freewriting** you will have a topic in mind when you start writing. First, write your topic at the top of the page. Then, for two to four minutes, write down everything that comes to mind with regard to your chosen topic. If you run out of ideas, rewrite the last idea in different ways until another fresh idea comes into your mind.

When your allotted time is up, look over what you have written. Cross out ideas that do not directly relate to your topic. Add new ones if necessary. Then number the ideas in some kind of logical order. Rewrite these in proper sentence form. You now have the points for the body of your paragraph.

BRAINSTORMING

The idea behind **brainstorming** is to ask yourself specific questions regarding your topic. Start these questions with "Who?" or "What?" and then with "How?", "When?", "Where?", and "Why?" Follow the same pattern as you did for focused freewriting outlined above. Be sure to set a time limit. Start asking the six questions, and write down your answers. When your allotted time is up, review your answers. Choose your topic sentence and write it down. Then decide which of your brainstorming ideas are most closely related to your topic sentence. Rewrite these ideas in proper sentence form, and begin writing the body of your paragraph.

11.4   ORGANIZING THE BODY OF YOUR PARAGRAPH

Now that you have developed your topic sentence and the points you are going to discuss in the paragraph, it is necessary to organize your points. There are three common ways of doing this:

1. *Logical order.* Start at one point and move logically to the next. This method is often used when one point must be explained for the next to make sense. This method could be used in a paragraph describing a person from head to toe, or from toe to head.

2. *Chronological order.* This is a way of organizing your points according to time, by moving from the start to the finish. This method is used frequently in narration and instructional paragraphs.

3. *Moving from a general statement to particular examples or details.* This method starts with a general statement made in your topic sentence and moves to details and/or examples in the points of the paragraph.

With all of these methods of organization, the use of transitional words helps to make sure that your points flow smoothly from one sentence to the next (see Module 10).

UNITY

Always check to make sure that all the sentences in your paragraph are about one main idea. Look at each sentence carefully and ask yourself the questions, "Does this sentence relate to the main idea in the topic sentence?" and "How?" You should be able to show exactly how each sentence in your paragraph relates directly back to your topic sentence.

When all the sentences in a paragraph are about one main idea, we say that the paragraph has **unity**, or oneness. Here is an example of a unified paragraph:

> The Amazon is by far the greatest river in South America. This enormous river flows about 6,500 kilometres across northern Brazil to the Atlantic Ocean. Nearly half of the water in South America flows through the Amazon system. As well as being the longest river, the Amazon is also the biggest. It contains more water than the Nile, the Mississippi, and the Yangtze together. The Amazon is so powerful that 300 kilometres out at sea, the ocean is still muddy from the topsoil carried by the river.

1. *The Amazon is by far the greatest river in South America* is the topic sentence in the paragraph.

2. The main idea is that the Amazon is the greatest river in South America.

3. Moving from a general statement to particular details is the method of organization used.

COHERENCE

It is very important to know and understand the difference between unity and coherence. Unity means that each sentence in a paragraph must relate directly back to the topic sentence by related ideas. **Coherence** means that each sentence must relate to its predecessor by both related ideas and mechanical devices.

Although both unity and coherence are achieved through the ideas being discussed or talked about, there are also mechanical and grammatical means of achieving both. The question now becomes, "How does one achieve coherence?" Here is how:

1. *Synonyms*—Instead of *leaves* in every sentence, for example, you could change this noun to *foliage* or *greenery* or *verdure*. Instead of repeating the proper noun *Shakespeare*, you can say *the dramatist*, *the playwright*, *the poet*, *the bard*, or *the writer*. After you have used all the synonyms possible, you then return to *leaves* or to *Shakespeare*.

2. *Pronoun reference*—Instead of repeating *Billy the Kid*, you can use a pronoun, such as *he*, *his*, *him*, and thus avoid the repetition. This will give you variety, thereby avoiding monotony for the reader.

3. *Repetition*—Sometimes repetition is unavoidable, but the general rule is: Avoid repetition whenever possible; use it only for emphasis. Too much repetition will make your writing appear juvenile and will result in the one thing you want to avoid: monotony.

4. *Transitional words* (also known as connectives)—Words like *as a result*, *consequently*, *hence*, *however*, *therefore*, *thus*, and *soon* will help link your ideas, sentence by sentence, and thus greatly enhance both unity and coherence.

> *NOTE:* Transitional words, when placed between two principal clauses, are preceded by a semicolon (;) and followed by a comma (,). See Modules 8 and 10.

■ **Examples:**

    a) I am sick; consequently, I cannot go out.

    b) I love the spring; however, I hate winter.

    c) My sister warned me; moreover, I intend to heed her warning.

Very briefly, then, here are the guides to effective paragraph writing:

1. Have a good opening sentence that captures the attention of your reader. This is often your topic sentence.

2. Maintain unity throughout.

3. Maintain coherence throughout.

4. Have variety in your sentence structure.

5. Have a good closing or summarizing sentence, one that knits everything together, or one that comments on what you have said in the paragraph.

VARIETY IN SENTENCE STRUCTURE

Now that you know about the main ingredients of any paragraph—topic sentence, body, and summarizing sentence—let us look at another way to make your paragraphs more interesting.

Variety has been called "the spice of life," mainly because it avoids monotony and boredom. You can achieve variety in your writing in several ways:

1. If possible, use different types of sentences according to your purpose. Mix all or any combination of assertive, interrogative, imperative, and exclamatory sentences. But do not force the use of any of these, simply to achieve variety. They should fit easily into what you write.

■ **Examples:**

I am going home.	(assertive)
Is she ready yet?	(interrogative)
Move quickly.	(imperative)
What a surprise!	(exclamatory)

2. Try to avoid starting every sentence with normal syntax (word order). Instead of beginning every sentence with a subject and verb, try beginning with an adverb, prepositional phrase, verbal phrase, or subordinate clause. Also, use different formats: natural, inverted, and split (see Module 9).

3. Use short, medium, and long sentences. A variety of different clausal structures will achieve this. Use simple, compound, complex, and compound-complex sentences (see Module 8).

11.5   THE SUMMARIZING SENTENCE

The final part of the paragraph is the summarizing sentence. The summarizing sentence can do one of two things: it can either sum up what you have already said or it can comment on what you have discussed in the paragraph. It makes your paragraph complete and unified.

■ **Examples:**

> Nothing disturbed the tranquillity that morning at Horseshoe Bay. The sailboat lay anchored without a movement. Along the curving shoreline, the birds sang sweetly in the trees. The morning sun shone brightly from a cloudless sky. Everything looked promising for a glorious day.

The final sentence makes the paragraph completely unified by commenting on what was discussed in the paragraph. It concludes or finishes the discussion. Above all, it does not just suddenly stop the paragraph in mid-air, so to speak.

11.6 THE CHECKLIST

We have now covered all the aspects of a paragraph. Here is a checklist to use for making sure that you have written a proper paragraph.

Did you:

1. Narrow your topic according to the purpose and the audience?

2. Write a proper topic sentence?

3. Freewrite or brainstorm to generate ideas?

4. Select and arrange your ideas according to the organizational methods mentioned?

5. Check for unity, coherence, and sentence variety?

6. Conclude your paragraph?

7. Proofread for grammar, spelling, and compositional errors?

EXERCISE 11.1

Write a paragraph that discusses your future job prospects. On a separate page, practice freewriting and brainstorming. Develop a paragraph outline showing the topic sentence, the supporting sentences, and the summary as concluding statement. Test your paragraph against the checklist in section 11.6. Write your final version of your paragraph in the space provided.

Suggestions:

_____

_____

_____

_____

_____

_____

Practice:

_____

_____

_____

_____

_____

_____

_____

_____

_____

_____

_____

_____

Final:

_____

_____

_____

_____

_____

_____

_____

_____

_____

_____

_____

_____

_____

EXERCISE 11.2

Not many people live in Antarctica. Five of the following sentences explain why this is the case. Cross out the other two.

1. Not a single tree or plant grows in Antarctica.

2. The first person to cross the Antarctic Circle was Captain James Cook.

3. Antarctica is one of the loneliest and most desolate places in the world.

4. No region on earth is as cold as Antarctica.

5. No one has ever lived in Antarctica except for a few scientists and explorers.

6. All but a very small part of Antarctica is permanently covered with thick ice.

7. Antarctica is the fifth largest continent.

A. Which sentence will make the best topic sentence? Why? Explain in a sentence.

_____

_____

_____

_____

B. Write a paragraph using as many of the remaining sentences as possible, placing them in order.

_____

_____

_____

_____

_____

_____

_____

_____

_____

_____

_____

_____

EXERCISE 11.3

For each of the following topic sentences, suggest a likely purpose and method of organization.

1. My grandfather is the wisest man I know.

   Purpose:

   _____

   Method of organization:

   _____

2. Last week I was involved in a car accident.

   Purpose:

   _____

   Method of organization:

   _____

3. In order to paint a room properly, there are certain things you must do to prepare the room.

Purpose:

_____

Method of organization:

_____

4. The first day of college was the most hectic day of my life.

Purpose:

_____

Method of organization:

_____

5. When it comes time to clip your cat's claws, there are certain precautions you must take for your own safety.

Purpose:

_____

Method of organization:

_____

EXERCISE 11.4

Read the following paragraph:

[1]How gorgeous was his broad hat with the long, flowing plume. [2]On mornings when I awoke very early, I could see it without raising my head from the pillow. [3]One of the greatest impressions for good made upon me when I was very small came from a picture of the _Blue Boy_ which mother hung on my bedroom wall directly opposite my bed. [4]It had a heavy, gilt frame. [5]Above my head on the wall was another masterpiece—_The Horse Fair_. [6]No single thing had such an influence on my boyhood as that picture, and I thank my mother for it—and the artist. [7]The clear, honest eyes looked straight at me and, sometimes, when I had been naughty the day before, I could hardly face them. [8]How bravely and proudly he stood among the wild surroundings of rocky hillside and dark clouds. [9]We were friends—this little aristocrat of a past age and I. [10]I liked his blue suit with the big bows at the knees and on his shoes, and the white trimming of collar and cuffs.

In full, correct sentences, answer the following questions. Explain your answer. Use the numbers at the beginning of each sentence for easy reference.

1. Does this paragraph tell a story, describe, or explain/inform?

_____

2. Which sentence would you choose for the topic sentence? Why?

_____

_____

3. Which sentence would you choose for the summary sentence? Why?

_____

_____

4. Which sentence disregards unity? How?

_____

_____

5. Which sentence introduces unnecessary detail? Explain your answer.

_____

_____

6. Which sentence should come before the other in the paragraph—sentence 8 or sentence 2? Why?

_____

_____

EXERCISE 11.5

In the space provided, write a paragraph of *approximately 150 words* in which you describe in detail the importance of communication skills in your field of study. Try to include some sentences using more advanced punctuation, like the semi-colon and the colon, as well as colourful adjectives and adverbs. Make it interesting to the reader. Because good writing means that you must write a first draft and then edit it for unity, coherence, and precision, include your first draft and your final, revised version.

Outline:

_____

_____

_____

_____

_____

Topic sentence:

_____

_____

_____

Supporting sentences:

_____

_____

_____

_____

_____

_____

First Draft

_____

_____

_____

_____

_____

_____

_____

_____

_____

_____

_____

_____

_____

_____

_____

_____

_____

_____

_____

_____

_____

_____

_____

_____

_____

_____

Final, Revised Version

_____

_____

_____

_____

_____

_____

_____

_____

_____

_____

_____

_____

_____

_____

EXERCISE 11.6

In the space provided below, write a six- or seven-sentence paragraph using one of the following as your first sentence. Be sure each of your sentences is complete and that you use singular and plural words correctly. Include at least two compound, two complex, and one compound-complex sentence in your paragraph.

1. *Whenever I try to study, I am usually distracted by several things.*

2. *I must do several things before I can get ready to come to class.*

3. *Students must fulfil several requirements before being accepted into a post-secondary program.*

_____

_____

_____

_____

_____

_____

_____

_____

_____

NOTES

NOTES

NOTES

NOTES

NOTES

NOTES

NOTES

NOTES

NOTES

NOTES

NOTES

NOTES

NOTES

NOTES

To the owner of this book

We hope that you have enjoyed *Foundations of Canadian College English,* and we would like to know as much about your experiences with this text as you would care to offer. Only through your comments and those of others can we learn how to make this a better text for future readers.

School _____ Your instructor's name _____

Course _____ Was the text required? _____ Recommended? _____

1. What did you like the most about *Foundations of Canadian College English?*

_____

_____

_____

2. How useful was this text for your course?

_____

_____

_____

3. Do you have any recommendations for ways to improve the next edition of this text?

_____

_____

_____

4. In the space below or in a separate letter, please write any other comments you have about the book. (For example, please feel free to comment on reading level, writing style, terminology, design features, and learning aids.)

_____

_____

_____

_____

Optional

Your name _____ Date _____

May Nelson Canada quote you, either in promotion for *Foundations of Canadian College English* or in future publishing ventures?

Yes _____ No _____

Thanks!

- - - - - - - - - - - FOLD HERE - - - - - - - - - - -

TAPE SHUT

TAPE SHUT

MAIL ⟫ POSTE
Canada Post Corporation
Société canadienne des postes
Postage paid   Port payé
if mailed in Canada si posté au Canada
Business Reply **Réponse d'affaires**
0066102399   **01**

0066102399-M1K5G4-BR01

Nelson

Nelson Canada
Market and Product Development
1120 Birchmount Rd.
Scarborough, ON M1K 9Z9

PLEASE TAPE SHUT. DO NOT STAPLE.